Prolog Wizard
A Wiley Programmer's Reference

Prolog Wizard
A Wiley Programmer's Reference

Dennis L. Foster

John Wiley & Sons, Inc.
New York • Chichester • Brisbane • Toronto • Singapore

Publisher: Stephen Kippur
Editor: Therese A. Zak
Managing Editor: Andrew B. Hoffer
Electronic Production Services: The Publisher's Network

This publication is designed to provide accurate and authoritative information in regard to the subject matter covered. It is sold with the understanding that the publisher is not engaged in rendering professional advice. If professional advice or other expert assistance is required, the services of a competent professional person should be sought.

Turbo is a registered trademark of Borland, Inc.

Library of Congress Cataloging-in-Publication Data

Foster, Dennis L.
   Prolog wizard.

   1. Prolog (Computer program language)
I. Title.
QA76.3.P76F67   1987   005.13'3   87-2082
ISBN 0-471-85348-8

Printed in the United States of America

87 88 10 9 8 7 6 5 4 3 2 1

Related Titles of Interest from John Wiley & Sons

Harmon & King	*Expert Systems: Artificial Intelligence in Business*
Sawyer & Foster	*Programming Expert Systems in Pascal*
Sawyer & Foster	*Programming Expert Systems in Modula-2*
Wiener	*Modula-2 Wizard: A Wiley Programmer's Reference*
Ford & Wiener	*Modula-2: A Software Development Approach*
Miller & Quilici	*C Programming Language: An Applied Perspective*
Schwaderer	*C Wizard's Programming Reference*
Crandall	*Pascal Applications for the Sciences*
Walden	*File Formats for Popular PC Software: A Programmer's Reference*
Stern	*Flowcharting: A Tool for Understanding Computer Logic*
Ashley & Fernandez	*PC DOS, 2nd Edition*
Winfield	*The Complete Forth*
Ashley, Fernandez & Beamesderfer	*JCL for IBM VSE Systems: A Self-Teaching Guide*
Morse & Albert	*The 80286 Architecture*
Morse, Albert & Isaacson	*The 80386 Architecture*
Fernandez, Tabler & Ashley	*6502 Assembly Language Programming*
Skinner	*An Introduction to Assembly Language Programming for the 8086 Family*
Ashley & Fernandez	*COBOL Wizard: A Wiley Programmer's Reference*
Ashley & Fernandez	*COBOL for Microcomputers*
Ashley	*Structured COBOL*
Tabler	*IBM PC Assembly Language*
DeWitt	*Hires/Double Hires Graphics for the Apple IIC and Apple II Family*
DeWitt	*Art and Graphics on the Apple II/IIC*
Finkel & Brown	*Data File Programming in Basic*
Brown & Finkel	*IBM PC Data File Programming*

Contents

Preface

From the time the first electronic thinking machines were on the drawing board, system designers have long argued the question of whether the proposed devices should compute or reason. Because military applications have often been pressing, the "compute" school usually took the upper hand. Nonetheless, a few undaunted logicians persevered in their quest for a machine that reasons.

Alain Colmerauer, a programmer at the University of Marseilles, inherited their zeal. The hallmark of his adventure was the development in 1971 of an extraordinary high-level language for "programming in logic." Colmerauer and his colleagues, Robert Kowalski and Phillipe Roussel, based the new language on the premise that a computer can draw inferences as efficiently as it can calculate sums.

Unlike conventional computer languages, the new syntax was not designed primarily to add and subtract numbers, but to process symbolic representations of reality. It dealt with empirical associations underlying the behavior of concepts and events. Moreover, conventional programs were deterministic; they followed the same set of steps each time they were executed. In contrast, a program written in the new instruction set developed its own execution path each time it attempted to solve a new problem.

The new language, Prolog, was first designed to process natural language. It is for this reason that most versions of Prolog in use today are *conversational* in nature; they rely on ordinary words and phrases, and they interact with their users much like a Greek oracle carrying on a conversation with a wisdom-seeking pilgrim.

Since its commercial introduction in 1972, Prolog has attracted widespread interest as an artificial intelligence (AI) development tool among programmers and end-users alike. With the current excitement over AI and expert systems, Prolog tools are more popular than ever. Borland International's introduction of its superlative Turbo Prolog for the IBM PC is unquestionably a milestone in the dissemination of Prolog tools to the general public. Earlier Prolog releases were designed to run on DEC mini/microsystems and CP/M-based microcomputers.

Commonly termed an AI language, Prolog is widely used in the design of expert systems and other rule-based applications, such as dynamic relational databases, conversational user interfaces, human language interpreters, and computer-assisted instruction.

This book is not a primer or tutorial, but rather a programmer's comprehensive reference guide. Designed for quick access and easy interpretation, this high-level resource provides concise, detailed information for designing, organizing, trouble-shooting, and debugging. The emphasis is clearly on Turbo Prolog, but the scope is broad enough to include other major Prolog releases, namely, DEC Prolog and MicroProlog. Programmers already conversant in other versions of Prolog and anxious to translate their know-how into Turbo will find this book particularly useful.

Even though this guide is not tutorial in nature, to programmers knowledgeable in any language, it offers insight into the underlying concepts, syntax, and practical applications that make Turbo Prolog and its precursors unique among automation-authoring tools.

Acknowledgments

I would like to acknowledge and thank the following parties for their respective contributions: Susan Murany, for research and technical assistance; Borland International, for technical support; Therese Zak and Theron Shreve, for editorial guidance; Mike Larsen and Elizabeth Pomada, for being my literary agents; and, as always, my wife Dawn, simply for being.

How to Use This Book

This book is organized into six sections, including a set of appendixes.

Section 1, "Prolog Overview," focuses on the construction of facts, objects, and rules in the light of Prolog syntax and Turbo Prolog construction.

Section 2, "Program Design and Construction," discusses the organization of program listings and elaborates on techniques for controlling execution. This section focuses on backtracking and the use of two run-time events, cut (!) and fail, to influence the decision tree.

Section 3, "The Built-in Predicates," explains the predefined predicates, offering tips for their use and describing potential hazards. The emphasis is on Turbo Prolog, but standard Prolog correlates are also explained, where appropriate.

Section 4, "Input/Output," is devoted to file creation and access, highlighting techniques for writing to and reading from Prolog files in RAM or on disk.

Section 5, "Special Effects," focuses on graphics and sound and demonstrates how to enhance Turbo Prolog programs with video attributes, windowing techniques, and Turtle Graphics.

The final section is a set of appendixes which include an ASCII code reference chart, a quick-reference guide to the built-in predicates and goals, a Prolog-to-Turbo Prolog conversion chart, graphics and sound values in tabular form, and a Turbo Prolog language summary. You will also find a tear-out reference card containing two figures and a duplicate of the important parts of the appendixes. Since the book is organized for quick access, it covers a great deal of detail but little tutorial information. After all, a broad discussion of expert systems, knowledge engineering, and heuristic logic is well beyond the scope of a programmer's reference guide.

Necessarily, there is a great deal of redundancy throughout the book in order to tell as complete a story as possible about each encyclopedic reference. A typical reader might possess a background in a structured high-level language such as C, Pascal, or Modula-2. However, even the enthusiast familiar with a learning language such as BASIC, Turtle Graphics, or Pilot should find this reference guide endurable. One might bear in mind that Prolog was first devised with the idea that uninitiated users would be able to develop useful applications without previous programming credentials.

The terminology of AI in general and Prolog in specific varies from one source to another. For consistency and clarity, we have settled on the following usages throughout this book:

The adjective *standard* is used only to describe predicates that are common to most versions of Prolog. To describe a predefined facility unique to one version, we use the preferred adjective *built-in*.

Throughout this book, we use the term *argument* to refer to the collective objects attached to a predicate in a Prolog or Turbo Prolog clause. In other words, the entire collection of phonemes enclosed within the parentheses following a predicate is considered to be *the argument*.

Any phoneme or symbol used in a Prolog or Turbo Prolog program is considered an *atom,* and any phoneme appearing within parentheses in an argument is technically an *object*.

We have adopted this terminology simply because it is most familiar to expert systems developers. After all, it was to develop expert systems that Prolog and its immensely popular stepchild, Turbo Prolog, were originally created.

Prolog Wizard
A Wiley Programmer's Reference

Prolog Overview

- **Introduction**
- **Facts**
- **Objects**
- **Domains**
- **Relations**
- **Variables**
- **Predicates**
- **Questions**
- **Rules**
- **Clauses**
- **Goals**
- **Operators**
- **Lists**

Introduction

The idea of programming in Prolog is to mimic the heuristic processes that underlie human problem solving. A Prolog program is thus a *rule-based system*, or RBS. The programmer expresses knowledge in the form of facts and rules; on execution, the program pursues a predefined goal, applying the rules to the appropriate factual expressions until it arrives at a feasible solution. In effect, the rule-based system formulates various alternative approaches to a stated problem, then tests the candidate solutions to fulfill its goal.

The three primary components of all Prolog programs are *facts, rules,* and *goals*. The facts and rules which translate human expertise into machine-processable symbols represent the rule-based system's *knowledge base*.

To visualize a Prolog program in action, consider the heuristics followed by a commodities trading expert advising an investor when to buy and sell futures. A classic case is the series of event behaviors that result from rising or declining interest rates and their eventual effect on commodities futures. The expert's reasoning may be that in a period of declining interest rates, real estate sales increase exponentially, creating demand in the housing market. As the supply of available homes dwindles, new home construction begins to soar. Lumber mills are generally idle except during times of peak demand, so the existing supply of seasoned lumber is quickly exhausted. The resulting shortage drives lumber prices up.

Conversely, when interest rates rise, real estate sales drop, a housing surplus develops, new home construction declines, and lumber mills, which were active while construction was soaring, produce a new surplus, driving the price of lumber down.

Each of these behaviors can be expressed as contingency relationships, or rules, between facts. A Prolog program is made up of facts defining the relations between objects, as well as rules which govern the contingencies or precedence relationships among different facts. For instance, the fact that there is (or will be) a lumber shortage may be expressed as follows:

```
supply(lumber,shortage)
```

In this expression, supply is the relation, and lumber and shortage are objects. More precisely, they are the values assigned to the objects they represent. Think of the actual objects as being commodity and condition, with lumber being the value of commodity and shortage being the value of condition:

```
supply(commodities,condition)
supply(lumber,shortage)
```

In other words, the relation supply pertains to all commodities and conditions in general, and to lumber and shortage in particular. The relation supply is referred to as the *predicate*, and the list of objects or values between the round brackets is the *argument*.

To distinguish these symbolic representations of reality from the quantitative data of a traditional program language, a Prolog fact is referred to as *assertive data*. In our sample fact, we are asserting lumber as the value of commodities, and shortage as the value of condition.

A Prolog rule consists of one or more if...then relationships. Consider, for instance, the rule that there will be a shortage of lumber if residential construction is up. This expression may be written as follows:

```
supply(lumber,shortage) if construction(residential,up)
```

Each half of the rule is a factual expression. The fact in the first part is the *conclusion*, and the fact that follows the if is the *premise*.

When a Prolog program attempts to solve a problem, it tests the conclusions and premises of the various rules contained in the listing until an unobstructed path is found to satisfy the goal. It also solves for any variables stated in the goal. Assume that a commodities trading program contains the following facts:

```
price(lumber, "will rise")
price(lumber, "will decline")
price(lumber, "will remain unchanged")
```

Each fact, or *clause,* contains a specific set of *legal values* for the objects in the argument. The actual objects might be commodity and action.

A goal is specified at execution: for example,

```
price(lumber,X)
```

The variable we are trying to solve is *X:* that is, the value which represents the predicted price action for the commodity lumber. Prolog processes all the rules in our database to determine which value of *X* is valid based on the new data we assert: for example, the current rate of interest.

Here are some other rules we might include in our commodities trading program:

```
supply(lumber,surplus) if construction(residential,down).
construction(residential,up) if sales(real_estate,up).
construction(residential,down) if sales(real_estate,down).
sales(real_estate,up) if trend(interest_rates,down).
sales(real_estate,down) if trend(interest_rates,up).
price(lumber,"will rise") if supply(lumber,shortage).
price(lumber,"will decline") if supply(lumber,surplus).
```

At this point, Prolog doesn't know whether interest rates are up or down, so the operator must supply the data at run-time. Based on the input value (either up or down), Prolog will find a solution to the goal.

```
price(lumber,X)
```

Our program might include a clause like the following one to display the solution in the form of a complete sentence.

```
write("The price of lumber",X).
```

Let's say the operator tells Prolog that interest rates are down. Based on the heuristic rules we defined earlier, the program would predict:

```
The price of lumber will rise.
```

Facts

A *fact* consists of one or more objects and a relation, expressed in the following format:

```
relation(object,object...object)
```

Facts may be used to list clauses or state goals in a Turbo Prolog listing.

Examples:

```
patient(smith)
predisposing_factors(weight,blood_pressure,origin)
employee("last name","first name","social security no")
```

Hazards:

The first component of a factual expression is the relation, which must begin with a lower-case letter. A predicate, clause, or goal may not begin with a symbol (other than the underscore character), number, or punctuation mark.

Figure 1.1 illustrates the differences in syntax among Turbo Prolog, DEC Prolog, and MicroProlog.

Turbo Prolog	DEC Prolog	MicroProlog
`patient(male,57).`	`patient(male,57).`	`((patient male 57))`
`wine(zinfandel,red).`	`wine(zinfandel,red).`	`((wine zinfandel red))`
`moves(blk,pawn,K4).`	`moves(blk,pawn,K4).`	`((moves blk pawn K4))`
`book(author,title)`	`book(author,title).`	`((book author title))`

Figure 1.1 Examples of factual expressions in the syntaxes of different versions of Prolog

In DEC Prolog, a period must be added to the end of every factual expression. In Turbo Prolog, a period appears at the end of a clause, a rule, or a goal. In a fact used as a predicate declaration, a period is not used.

The relation in a fact is referred to as the *predicate*, and collectively, the objects enclosed in round brackets are the *argument*.

In MicroProlog, the relation and objects are listed without punctuation and enclosed in double round brackets. The first item is always interpreted as the relation.

Objects

An *object name* (or *atom*) may consist of any number of alpha or numeric characters. In Turbo Prolog, the initial character depends on the object's declared domain.

The underscore character may be used for legibility and clarity in any object name, but blank spaces may only be used in objects enclosed in double quotation marks (i.e., strings).

Examples:

```
budget
5000
fixed__price
"medical history"
```

A *compound object* is a primary object consisting of one or more subobjects and is expressed in the following format:

```
object(subobject,subobject...subobject)
```

A subobject may also be a compound object with additionally ordered subobjects.

Examples:

```
ekg(normal,elevated_st)
symptom(pain(chest,abdomen,arm))
application(education,business(word_processing,accounting))
```

Hazards:

In Turbo Prolog, the object domain stipulates the permissible characters that may be used in the name of an object. Whereas in standard versions of Prolog an object may be only a constant or an integer, in Turbo Prolog any of six standard domain types may apply. For instance, an object in the symbol domain must begin with a lower-case letter, or else it must begin and end with double quotation marks. An object with an initial upper-case character is always interpreted as a variable.

Functors

A *functor* is the first atom, or object name, in a compound object. Consider the compound object in the following factual expression:

```
wines(white,red(zinfandel,burgundy))
```

The functor in the compound object is red, describing the commonality among the sub-objects zinfandel and burgundy.

Domains

In Turbo Prolog, a domain must be declared for each object category stated in the predicate declaration. Figure 1.2 illustrates the six domain types.

```
symbol     string     char     integer     real     file
```

Figure 1.2 The six domain types

The object domains are declared at the front of the Turbo Prolog listing. Figure 1.3 illustrates a domain declaration.

```
domains

    patient, complaint, ekg   = symbol

    age, weight               = integer

    red_blood_cell_count      = real
```

Figure 1.3 Example of a Turbo Prolog domain declaration

Symbol

An object in the Turbo Prolog symbol domain may consist of any combination of alphanumeric characters, but the initial character must be a lower-case letter. No blank spaces are permitted, but the underscore character may be used for legibility and clarity, except as the first character.

Examples:

```
item
id15012
account_number
```

Alternatively, the object may begin and end with double quotation marks, permitting the use of an initial upper-case character or blank spaces within the object name. In general, any combination of spaces and alphanumeric characters may be inserted between the double quotation marks.

Examples:

"o-ring seal"
"Challenger"
"lift off"

Exercise care that you do not confuse objects of the symbol domain enclosed in double quotation marks with objects of the string domain.

String

An object in the string domain must begin and end with double quotation marks. Blank spaces (white space) may be used for legibility and clarity, and either alpha or numeric characters may be used.

Examples:

"EKG tracing"
"ischemic heart disease"

Char

An object in the char domain must consist of a character inserted between beginning and ending single quotation marks.

Examples:

'x'
'/'
'v'

Integer

An object in the integer domain may not be less than $-32,768$ nor greater than $32,767$.

Examples:

512
-6667

Real

All other numerical object names, including those with decimals and exponents, belong to the real domain.

Examples:

```
52580
−94181
72.05
−720e318
```

File

In a program involving input/output with a disk file, a file domain is declared to define a symbolic name, or synonym. After the file has been opened, all subsequent read and write operations identify the file by its symbolic name and not its DOS filename.

Examples:

```
openread(diskfile, "current.dat")
```

This clause opens a file whose DOS name is current.dat for reading. The symbolic name diskfile will be used to read data from the file.

Examples:

```
readdevice(diskfile),
readln(Line1).
```

In this instance, the file domain would be declared as follows:

```
file = diskfile
```

Figure 1.4 illustrates the construction of object names belonging to the standard Turbo Prolog domains.

Hazards:

Avoid using a backslash (\ ) in an object of the char or string domain. Turbo Prolog interprets a backslash followed by a number as an ASCII code. If you require the backslash character in a string, for example, to identify a DOS subdirectory, use two backslashes.

DEC Prolog

In DEC Prolog, domains are not declared. An object or relation may be either an atom or an integer. An atom is any character string beginning with a lower-case letter and including :- (the rule notation for if).

Objects may be composed of strings enclosed in double quotation marks or single characters enclosed in single quotation marks.

Figure 1.4 illustrates differences in construction among objects of varying Turbo Prolog domain types.

```
Object                          Domain
─────────────────────────────────────────
365                             integer

annual_sales                    symbol

"E Coli"                        string

112.75                          real

'r'                             char
```

Figure 1.4 Examples of Turbo Prolog object names

Hazards:

A domain declaration normally pertains only to the module in which the declaration is made. If transfer is made to another, separately compiled module, the declaration becomes null immediately upon transfer of control.

A *global domain* is valid for objects stated in any successive module and not merely in the module in which the declaration appears. The declaration is identical to that for standard domains. Figure 1.5 illustrates a global domain declaration.

```
global domains

    part_number    = real

    description    = string
```

Figure 1.5 Examples of a global domain declaration in Turbo Prolog

Relations

A *relation* may consist of any alphanumeric string and must always begin with a lower-case letter. Its function is to describe the relationship between the objects named in the argument of a fact. In all versions of Prolog, the first atom, or name, in a fact is always interpreted as the relation.

In both objects and relations, the underscore character may be used for legibility and clarity, except as the first character.

Examples:

```
directory_maximum(filenames,1024)
part(number,brand,description,price)
has_had(patient,hepatitis_B)
stipulates(contract,fixed_price)
```

Variables

A Prolog variable may be known or anonymous. When a program is executed, Prolog solves for any known variables stated in a goal, but it ignores any anonymous variables.

Known

A *known variable* is any object name whose initial character is an upper-case letter. In both Turbo Prolog and DEC Prolog, any atom beginning with a capital letter is interpreted as a known variable.

Examples:

```
Part_number
Price
Recommended_action
```

Anonymous

In all versions of Prolog, an *anonymous variable* is represented by the underscore character used in place of a known variable when the referenced object is insignificant. Any object in the position where an anonymous variable appears will match. The effect is to ignore any objects in this position.

Figure 1.6 illustrates the use of known and anonymous variables in Turbo Prolog goals.

Expression	Variables	Type
part(pvc_valve,motocraft,Price)	Price	known
scores("Brown",_,Math)	_	anonymous
	Math	known
territory(Manager,35000)	Manager	known
flights(Seats,_,329,_)	_	anonymous
	Seats	known

Figure 1.6 Example uses of variables in Prolog goals

Free and Bound

A *free variable* is a variable whose value is unknown. A *bound variable* is a variable whose value has been determined by Prolog pursuant to a predefined goal.

A known variable is free until a match has been located in the argument of a clause. When a match is found, the variable becomes bound to the corresponding value. When backtracking occurs, the variable is again freed.

Variable Handling

The following example demonstrates how Prolog handles known and anonymous variables. Assume you have constructed a database for storing the title, starring actor, and release date of each film stored in a private collection. Your clauses might resemble the following examples.

Examples:

```
film("On the Waterfront","Marlon Brando",1954)
film("8 1/2","Marcello Mastroianni",1958)
film("The Godfather","Marlon Brando",1972)
```

To determine the starring actor in "8 1/2," the following goal may be used:

```
film("8 1/2",Star,_)
```

The variables are Star (known) and _ (anonymous). Prolog matches the known variable and ignores the anonymous variable—in this case, the release date—which is irrelevant to our inquiry. Prior to execution, Star is a free variable; that is, its value is unknown. When Prolog locates a match, the variable becomes bound to the corresponding value—in this case, "Marcello Mastroianni."

To determine the titles and release dates of films in which Marlon Brando was the starring actor, the following goal may be used:

```
film(Title,"Marlon Brando",Date)
```

Both variables—Title and Date—are known. Prolog matches the variables with all possible solutions, resulting in a list of titles and dates which have the atom "Marlon Brando" in common. The variable Title becomes bound to "On the Waterfront" and "The Godfather," and Date becomes bound to the integers 1954 and 1972.

Predicates

A *predicate* is the relation side of a factual expression. Each predicate used in a Prolog clause must be declared, based on the declared domain types for object names.

A predicate is declared in the form of a fact whose argument consists of objects whose domains were previously declared. Any relation used in a clause must first be declared as a predicate.

Examples:

```
patient(name,age,weight,blood_pressure)
market(territory,manager,sales)
genus(species,species,species)
```

Domain types must also be declared for all objects appearing in a predicate declaration. Figure 1.7 illustrates domain and predicate declarations.

```
Domains

    name                = symbol

    age, weight         = integer

    blood_pressure      = string

Predicates

    patient(name,age,weight,blood_pressure)
```

Figure 1.7 Examples of Turbo Prolog domain and predicate declarations

Global

In Turbo Prolog, unless otherwise specified, a predicate is valid only for the program module in which the declaration is made. If control is transferred to another, separately compiled module, Prolog will not recognize the predicate unless it has been redeclared.

A *global predicate* is valid for all successive modules beginning with the point at which the declaration is made. The following format is observed to declare a global predicate:

```
relation(object,object...object) – (f,f...f)(f,f...f)
```

The standard predicate declaration is appended with a description of the input/output flow. The value of f may be either i (input) or o (output).

Figure 1.8 illustrates a global predicate declaration.

```
global predicates
    patient(age,weight,blood_pressure) - (i,i,i)(o,o,o)
```

Figure 1.8 Example of a Turbo Prolog global predicate declaration

Questions

To pose a question in Turbo Prolog, the user simply tests a fact to see if it is true by stating the fact as a goal. If the test is positive, Turbo replies: TRUE. If the goal cannot be substantiated, a FALSE response is displayed.

The following example illustrates the inquiry method in Turbo Prolog.

```
GOAL: patient("Kendall",female)
TRUE
```

DEC Prolog and MicroProlog

In DEC Prolog, a question may be posed by prefixing a fact with ?-. A TRUE or FALSE response may be displayed.

Examples:

```
?-patient("Kendall",female).
```

In MicroProlog, an inquiry is preceded only by a question mark. If the fact fails, Prolog responds with a question mark. If the fact succeeds, no response is displayed.

Examples:

```
?((patient "Kendall" female))
```

A question requiring a printed response must be appended with the MicroProlog predicates to print (PP) and fail.

Examples:

?((patient Name female) (PP Name) (FAIL))

Rules

A Turbo Prolog rule consists of a conclusion and a premise expressed in the following general format:

relation(object) if
    relation(object).

Note the mandatory period at the end of the expression. Any number of objects may be included in the argument on either side of the rule, and the premise may include more than one fact.

Examples:

wine(label,vintage,red) if
    meal(salad,beef,dessert).
prescribe(ampicillin) if
    infection(patient,e_coli) and
    not_allergic(patient).
recommended(action,sell) if
    has_risen(stock,10) and
    has_declined(stock,5).

DEC Prolog

A rule in a DEC Prolog program uses the symbol :- to represent the if portion of the expression. For ease of conversion, Turbo Prolog also recognizes this notation in the construction of a rule.

Examples:

wine(vintage,label,red) :- meal(salad,beef,dessert).

Clauses

The facts and rules that constitute a Prolog program's knowledge base are known as *clauses*.

A clause is a factual expression with a declared predicate (relation) and an argument consisting of specific objects, or it can be a rule which includes such factual expressions in its premise and conclusion.

Examples:

```
patient("Kendall",female,24)
stock("Armco","30 Aug",89.25,"up",5)
buy(negociant) if province("Bordeaux").
```

In Turbo Prolog, clauses must be declared along with domains and predicates. Figure 1.9 illustrates their declarations.

```
domains
    brand,descr,part_number  = string
predicates
    part(brand,descr,part_number)
clauses
    part("Seagate","20mb hd","SE199").

    part("Mitsubishi","16k RAM","MI502").

    part("CDC","disk_drive","CD091").
```

Figure 1.9 Example of domain, predicate, and clause declarations in a Turbo Prolog listing

Goals

A goal is a fact or rule which Prolog seeks to satisfy by testing the facts and rules contained in the clauses section of the program. In Turbo Prolog, goals may be declared in the program listing or, if no goal is so declared, Prolog will prompt the user to enter a goal when executing a program.

Prolog seeks a match for any known variables stated in a goal.

A *compound goal* consists of two or more subgoals, both of which must be satisfied before Prolog may conclude the execution.

Examples:

```
patient("Kendall",female,Age)
wine(Varietal,with_lobster) and wine(Varietal,dry)
```

When a compound goal is declared, Turbo Prolog pursues each subgoal from left to right. In the example above, the program would first solve the variable Varietal to match with_lobster, bind the solution, then pursue a match with dry.

Turbo Prolog supports both internal and external goals. An external goal, supplied at run-time, will result in all solutions; an internal goal, declared in the program listing, will result in only the first solution found.

Multiple

A goal may consist of multiple facts, each of which will be satisfied in order of appearance. A comma must be used to separate each fact in the series, and a period must appear after the last fact. Figure 1.10 illustrates the declaration of a multiple goal.

```
goal

        price(lumber,Prediction),

        write("The Price of lumber, ",Prediction),

        nl.
```

Figure 1.10 Example of a multiple goal declaration in Turbo Prolog

In the illustration, the first fact in the multiple goal prompts Prolog to bind a value to the variable Prediction. The second fact uses the built-in predicate write to print the results of the search on the screen in a conversational expression. The final fact consists of the built-in predicate for the new-line character (nl).

An elegant technique for handling multiple goals is the description of a subroutine in the clauses declaration. The subroutine is written as a rule whose conclusion is the name of the goal and whose premise comprises the factual series.

Figure 1.11 illustrates a multiple goal described in the clause declaration.

```
domains

    commodity, action   = symbol

predicates

    price(commodity,action)

    analyze

goal

    analyze.

clauses

    analyze:-

        price(lumber,Prediction),

        write(The price of lumber ",Prediction),

        nl.
```

Figure 1.11 Example of a multiple goal constructed as a rule in Turbo Prolog

Operators

Prolog operators are divided into two classes: arithmetic and relational. The arithmetic operators include the symbols for addition, subtraction, multiplication, and division. In Turbo Prolog, if two integers are added, subtracted, or multiplied, the result will be an integer. However, if one of the operands in any of these operations is a real number, the result will always be real as well. The result of a division, whether the operands are integers or real numbers, is always real.

Arithmetic

All versions of Prolog support the following arithmetic operators, listed in order of priority of execution.

+   Add
−   Subtract
*   Multiply
/   Divide

Round brackets may be used to supply preference of execution in a compound expression. Consider, for example, the following equation:

```
S1 = 12/2+2
```

Prolog performs arithmetic with left-hand preference, so that the equation above is equivalent to

```
S1 = (12/2)+2
```

For more complex operations, trigonometric functions, and absolute values, Turbo Prolog supplies built-in predicates. Figure 1.12 illustrates several examples.

```
sqrt(Volume)              Square root of the variable bound
                              to Volume

log(X)                    Logarithm of X

ln(Y)                     Natural logarithm of Y

Len div Wid               Quotient of Len divided by Wid

abs(Balance)              Absolute value of the variable bound
                              to Balance

sin(T)                    Sine of T

cos(A)                    Cosine of A

tan(C)                    Tangent of C
```

Figure 1.12 Examples of Turbo Prolog arithmetic predicates

Relational

Turbo Prolog supports the following relational operators:

```
=     Equal to
>     Greater than
> =   Greater than or equal to
<     Less than
< =   Less than or equal to
< >   Not equal to
```

Relational operators pertain to alpha as well as numeric expressions.

Examples:

```
Expenses > Revenues
X < = Y
Player1 < > Player2
"Techmar" < "Teledyne"
```

When two objects in the symbol or string domain are compared, the characters in their names are converted to ASCII equivalents. The value of each character is tested against the relational operator, from left to right. Hence, strings beginning with a (ASCII decimal 97) are invariably less than strings beginning with c (ASCII decimal 99).

Lists

A Prolog *list* is an array of object names, or atoms, separated by commas and enclosed in square brackets. In Turbo Prolog, lists have the following format:

```
[member1,member2...memberN]
```

The members of the list may be any valid object names, but all the members must belong to the same declared domain.

Examples:

```
["Kendahl","Smith","Larsen"]
[495,512,424,570]
[income,expenses,net,cash_flow]
```

A domain must be declared for each list as well as for each object that is a member of a list. The domain for the list is the object name corresponding to its members, appended with an asterisk. The domain for the object name is the applicable Turbo Prolog domain. Figure 1.13 illustrates the domain declaration of a list and its objects.

```
domains

    custlist  = customer*

    customer  = string
```

Figure 1.13 Example of a list domain declaration in Turbo Prolog

Heads and Tails

A Prolog list has a *head*, normally the first element in the array, and a *tail* composed of the remaining elements. Consider the following example:

["Walsh","Montana","Clark","Craig"]

"Walsh" is the head of the list, and the tail is composed of "Montana," "Clark," and "Craig." To bind variables to the members of a list, a vertical bar is used to separate the variable representing the head from the variable representing the tail.

Examples:

```
[Coach|Team]
[A|B]
[Test_name|Lab_results]
```

If the first example pertained to the given list of names, the left-hand variable (Coach) would be bound to "Walsh," and the right-hand variable (Team) would be bound to the remaining members.

Figure 1.14 illustrates the use of variable binding to match the members of a Prolog list.

Variables	List	Binding
[A|B]	[appl,wp,acct,db]	A = appl
		B = [wp,acct,db]
[A,B|C]	[92,89,88,83,81]	A = 92
		B = 89
		C = [88,83,81]
[Stock,Trend,Amt]	["Altos","up","1/2"]	Stock = "Altos"
		Trend = "up"
		Amt = "1/2"

Figure 1.14 Examples of variable binding with Turbo Prolog lists

Program Design and Construction

- **Backtracking**
- **Modular Program Construction**
- **Program Construction with Turbo Prolog**

Backtracking

A Prolog program is constructed as a series of facts and rules. Consider the following small program storing the opening and closing prices of various commodities.

```
price(corn,1.85,1.65).
price(lumber,169.7,165.9).
price(silver,571.0,560).
price(eurodollars,94.27,94.29).
```

The output depends on the stipulated goal. For instance, one may request a listing for the first commodity in the database by specifying the goal:

```
price(X,Y,Z).
```

Prolog will evaluate the first clause, attempting to find a match for the variables X, Y, and Z. Finding a solution, it displays the values for X (commodity) as well as Y and Z (the prices). Real numbers are used for the prices in this example, but in some versions of Prolog, only integers are allowed. In our sample program, the following solution would be output:

```
X = corn, Y = 1.85, Z = 1.65
```

Prolog pursues a solution until the goal succeeds. If the goal fails, it backtracks and evaluates another clause. Backtracking continues in this fashion until the first solution is found to satisfy the current goal.

Backtracking, or backward chaining, is the heart of Prolog's unrelenting goal pursuit. Whenever Prolog is unable to satisfy a goal, backtracking is initiated. In backtracking, Prolog re-evaluates the goals that have been satisfied to that point and attempts to identify alternative solutions.

Backtracking takes place along the same execution path in which the initiating failure occurred. Hence, once Prolog has satisfied one goal, if a succeeding subgoal fails, backtracking will first seek to satisfy other subgoals until all the alternative pathways have been exhausted.

Backtracking is initiated spontaneously whenever a clause fails, but it may also be invoked intentionally to control program execution or output.

fail

To output all available solutions to a goal, one must force the goal to fail after a solution has been found. The built-in predicate fail is used for this purpose; it always fails, thus enforcing backtracking until all possible solutions have been exhausted. Assume we trail our goal with a fail predicate, as follows:

```
price(X,Y,Z), fail.
```

Forced to backtrack, Prolog outputs all possible values for *X*, *Y*, and *Z*:

```
X = corn, Y = 1.85, Z = 1.65;
X = lumber, Y = 169.7, Z = 165.9;
X = silver, Y = 571.0, Z = 560;
Y = eurodollars, Y = 94.27, Z = 94.29
```

The semicolon is the relational operator for or, denoting that four solutions are possible. However, if we specify the commodity, Prolog will return the price activity for that value only. Consider the following goal:

```
price(lumber,Y,Z).
```

In this case, only one solution is possible, so fail is unnecessary:

```
Y = 169.7   Z = 165.9
```

To obtain a listing of only the names of the commodities stored in the database, one may substitute an anonymous variable in the second and third positions of the argument. Prolog will ignore all values for *Y* and *Z* when it solves the goal:

```
price(X,_,_),fail.
```

The result is the following output.

```
X = corn
X = lumber
X = silver
X = eurodollars
```

A somewhat more cosmetic output is acheived with the built-in predicate write, which prints the value of a given variable on the console screen.

```
price(X,Y,Z),
write(X," Open: ",Y," Close: ",Z).
```

Each time Prolog outputs a solution, it will display the results in the following format:

```
lumber Open: 169.7   Close: 165.9
```

Note: In some versions of Prolog, single quotation marks, or apostrophes, are used to define a print string.

When rules are added to the database, the program is empowered to form conclusions and offer advice. For instance, in our sample commodities program, we might add the following rule:

```
Sell(X) :- price(X,Y,Z) and Z < Y
```

The :- symbol is the Prolog operator for if. In plain English, the rule states to advise a sell action if the closing price is lower than the opening price. Referring to our sample database, if we enforce backtracking with fail, Prolog would recommend:

```
Sell(corn)
Sell(lumber)
Sell(silver)
```

More precisely, it binds the objects corn, lumber, and silver to the variable *X*.

cut

Unless prohibited, backtracking may occur unintentionally. Moreover, it places demands on memory and compounds the amount of time required to solve a goal with complex relationships. To counter this possibility, a *cut*, indicated by an exclamation mark, inhibits backtracking. It always succeeds— and succeeds only once in the same place.

Consider, for instance, the following rule:

```
common(List1,List2,X) if
        member(X,List1) and member(X,List2).
```

The rule states that if a member, *X*, of List1 is also a member of *List2*, then *X* is common to both lists. The effect is to test whether a particular value is contained in two separate lists. For instance, the lists might represent the performance characteristics of different machines. If we instruct Prolog to find two machines with at least one characteristic in common, a multiplicity of solutions may result. In fact, an identical solution will be returned each time a characteristic is found to be a member of both lists. If two machines have seven characteristics in common, they will be paired seven times. To prohibit backtracking and return only the first solution, we may insert a cut (!) after the rule, as follows:

```
common(List1,List2,X) if
        member(X,List1) and member(X,List2),!.
```

The cut tells Prolog to cease pursuing the goal as soon as it finds the first possible solution.

Modular Program Construction

A rule consists of a conclusion, if, and a premise. The premise may consist of multiple clauses, each of which must succeed for the conclusion to succeed. Hence, the rule may be used as the instrument of modular program construction. Consider, as an example, the following rule:

```
display_prices:-
        price(X,Y,Z),
        write(X," Open: ",Y," Close: ",Z"),
        fail.
```

This rule has the effect of defining the clause display prices as an execution routine involving the steps whose clauses are contained in the premise. Hence, the conclusion display prices may be used as the name of a goal or as a clause in the premise of another rule. For instance, another rule might state:

```
recommendation:-
        display_prices,
        action,
        menu.
```

When the goal recommendation is pursued, the clause display prices will invoke its own set of clauses, all of which must succeed before the next clause, action, may be evaluated.

Program Construction with Turbo Prolog

Not by accident, Borland International's elegant and popular Turbo Prolog resembles Turbo Pascal as much as it resembles Prolog. Like Turbo Pascal, Turbo Prolog is highly structured and modular; it also incorporates many Turbo Pascal-like facilities for input/output, string handling, file handling, screen manipulation, graphics, and sound. Compare, for instance, the following Turbo Prolog clauses with comparable statements in Turbo Pascal:

```
write("Commodity: "),
readln(C).
```

Readers with even the slightest exposure to Pascal will realize immediately that the terms are identical in both languages. Besides phraseology and syntax, the two products have several other features in common: one is a superb compiler accessed by a multiwindow menu program and supported by a WordStar®-like screen editor; another is an economical price well within the reach of almost any computer user.

As with Turbo Pascal, a Turbo Prolog program must be entered in the form of a listing held in a file for compilation. In standard versions of Prolog, clauses may be entered in a conversational manner: Prolog displays a prompt (e.g., ?-) and the user keys in a fact or goal. In Turbo Prolog, the database of facts are usually stated in the appropriate section of the listing or stored in a file which can be read into memory at run-time. Thus the most conspicuous difference between Prolog and Turbo Prolog is that Prolog is primarily conversational, whereas Turbo Prolog is primarily structured.

Turbo Prolog can be "forced" to behave interactively by running a program with nothing but a goal, that is, with no declarations. When the *goal:* prompt is displayed in the Dialog window, the operator may enter factual expressions one by one, as in so-called pure Prolog.

Declarations

Superficially, a Turbo Prolog listing resembles a Pascal program in that certain elements of syntax must be declared at the top of the listing. In Pascal, one declares elements such as variables and type construction. In Turbo Prolog, one declares things like domains, predicates, goals, and clauses.

At a minimum, a Turbo Prolog listing must contain at least one predicate declaration for every user-defined predicate. A goal is mandatory for execution. If a goal is not declared in the program listing, Turbo will prompt the user to supply a goal when the run option is selected from the compiler menu.

Declarations are made in the following order:

```
domains
global domains
database
predicates
global predicates
goal
clauses
```

Figure 2.1 shows an algorithm of a typical Turbo Prolog program, demonstrating the order and construction of declarations.

```
domains

        declare symbol objects
        declare string objects
        declare char objects
        declare integer objects
        declare real objects
        declare symbolic filenames
        declare database objects

database

        database(object,object...object)

predicates

        declare predicates
```

(continued)

```
goal

    predicate(object,object...object).

clauses

    predicate(object):-
        predicate(object,object...object),
        predicate(object,object...object),
            .
            .
            .
        predicate(object,object...object).
    predicate(object):-
        predicate(object,object...object),
        predicate(object,object...object),
            .
            .
        predicate(object,object...object).
        .
        .
    predicate(object):-
        predicate(object,object...object),
        predicate(object,object...object),
            .
            .
        predicate(object,object...object).
```

Figure 2.1 Algorithm of a Turbo Prolog program

On compilation, a syntax error will be returned for every undeclared predicate devised by the programmer. Built-in predicates must not be not declared. Any name appearing in a predicate declaration will be interpreted as a user-defined predicate; if the name is one of the reserved Turbo Prolog names (e.g., readterm), a syntax error will result.

To enable new clauses to be added to the database of facts, a database must be declared. If the only facts to be evaluated are the ones listed in the clauses section, and no facts will be added or deleted, the database is not declared.

Normally, a domain or predicate declaration is only valid for the module in which the declaration appears. If control is transferred to another, separately compiled module, the declared domains and predicates will no longer be valid, unless they were originally declared in a global declaration.

The clauses declaration defines the clauses and rules that will be evaluated in the consultation.

Figure 2.2 illustrates the construction of a simple Turbo Prolog program. A domain is declared for every object appearing in the argument of a clause, but not for a predicate. A database is declared so that new facts may be asserted at run-time. A predicate declaration is made for every user-defined predicate, but not for built-in predicates like *write, readln,* or *asserta.*

```
domains
  object,value      = symbol
database
  trend(object,value)
predicates
  supply(object,value)
  construction(object,value)
  sales(object,value)
  price(object,value)
  prediction
  new_data
goal
  makewindow(1,7,7,"Lumber",0,0,12,46),
  prediction,
  new_data.
clauses
  supply(lumber,shortage) :-
        construction(residential,up).
  supply(lumber,surplus) :-
        construction(residential,down).
  supply(lumber,adequate) :-
        construction(residential,static).
  construction(residential,up) :-
        sales(real_estate,up).
  construction(residential,down) :-
        sales(real_estate,down).
  construction(residential,static) :-
        sales(real_estate,static).
  sales(real_estate,down) :-
        trend(interest_rates,a).
  sales(real_estate,up) :-
        trend(interest_rates,c).
  sales(real_estate,static) :-
        trend(interest_rates,b).
  price(lumber,"will rise") :-
        supply(lumber,shortage).
  price(lumber,"will decline") :-
        supply(lumber,surplus).
  price(lumber,"will remain unchanged") :-
        supply(lumber,adequate).
  prediction :-
        write("Are interest rates:"),nl,nl,
        write("  a.   13% or higher"),nl,
        write("  b.   10% to 12.9%"),nl,
        write("  c.   Below 10%"),nl,
        readln(X),
        asserta(trend(interest_rates,X)),
        price(_,Y),
        write("The price of lumber ",Y,"."),
        nl.
  new_data:-
        retract(trend(_,_)),
        fail,
        keypressed.
```

Figure 2.2 Construction of a simple Turbo Prolog program

Punctuation

A period must appear after each fact declared as a goal, clause, or rule. A rule always ends with a period, but when a series of facts is included in the premise, a comma must separate each fact from the others. The comma is interchangeable with *and*. A semicolon is used to denote *or* in a rule or domain declaration. Either *if* or *:-*, the standard Prolog atom, may be used to separate the premise from the conclusion.

Hence, the rule:

```
new_data if retract(attributes(_,_,_)) and fail.
```

is identical in meaning to:

```
new_data:-
        retract(attributes(_,_,_)),
        fail.
```

Double quotation marks are used to enclose a string value. In general, any characters appearing between the quotation marks will be interpreted as part of the string. A string value may be used in any object belonging to either the symbol domain or the string domain. Single quotation marks are used to enclose an object belonging to the char domain, that is, a single character.

The argument in a fact must be enclosed in round brackets (parentheses). All atoms appearing between the round brackets will be interpreted as the objects in the argument. In a compound object, a round bracket must begin and conclude each argument. Square brackets are used to enclose the members of a list.

Comments may be included in the listing by placing /* at the beginning of the comment and */ at the end. The following is an example of a Turbo Prolog comment.

```
/* Updates the Index File */
```

The characters enclosed in the comment markers will appear in the program listing, but they will be ignored on execution. Comments may be desirable to reference modules, explain an abstruse routine, or insert programming notes during the construction of a complex or lengthy application.

Figure 2.3 lists the Turbo Prolog punctuation characters.

(	begin argument
)	end argument
:-	if
,	and
.	end of fact or rule
"	begin/end string
'	begin/end character
[	begin list
]	end list
/*	begin comment
*/	end comment

Figure 2.3 Turbo Prolog punctuation characters

SECTION 3

The Built-in Predicates

- **Syntax**

Given sufficient memory, a Prolog program could be designed quite adequately using only clauses constructed with user-defined predicates. However, the presence of various, predefined predicates makes the design chore (and the compilation problem) all the more efficient. All versions of Prolog provide certain built-in predicates for input/output, string handling, and list processing. In addition, Borland International's immensely structured Turbo Prolog offers some exceptionally convenient facilities for video and sound attributes, disk procedures, and interfacing with DOS.

The built-in predicates are the Prolog correlate to the instruction set of a conventional high-level language: they are mnemonic symbols that facilitate program construction and aggregate machine-level execution. But unlike conventional programming instructions, Prolog predicates are used exclusively in factual expressions of the format:

```
relation(object,object...object).
```

Hence, technically, a built-in predicate is a relation that influences predefined object names and may take the form of an input line string, a video attribute, a disk file, or even a physical port designation.

Certain predicates are standard to all the major hybrids of Prolog, for example, *fail* and *asserta* (ADDCL in Micro-Prolog). Indeed, no language without at least these fundamental design facilities could rightly call itself Prolog by any stretch of its artificial imagination.

Because the built-in predicates have predefined effects, their names are reserved; they should not be used by the designer to construct customized atoms and expressions. Some terms, though not reserved, are restricted in Turbo Prolog, because they are synonymous with the names of built-in predicates. Treat these less severe, restricted atoms as if they were reserved.

A common cause of aberrant behavior in a user-defined clause is the use of a reserved or restricted term in a predicate or object name. When the term corresponds to a built-in predicate requiring a specified object domain, a syntax error is likely on compilation. However, because Turbo Prolog permits multiple predicate declarations, a restricted predicate used inadvertently as a user-defined predicate can produce seemingly bizarre results. Any syntax error resulting from a clause constructed with a user-defined predicate merits a crosscheck with the list of prohibited terms in Figure 3.1.

and	diagnostics	inkey
arctan	dir	isname
asserta	disk	keypressed
assertz	display	left
attribute	div	length
back	domains	line
beep	dot	ln
bios	edit	makewindow
bitand	editmsg	membyte
bitleft	eof	memword
bitright	existfile	mod
bitxor	exit	nl
bound	exp	nobreak
char_int	fail	not
check_cmpio	field_attr	nowarnings
check_determ	file_str	openappend
clauses	filemode	openmodify
clear_window	filepos	openread
closefile	findall	openwrite
code	flush	or
comline	forward	pencolor
concat	free	pendown
config	frontchar	penpos
consult	frontstr	penup
cos	fronttoken	port_byte
cursor	gotowindow	predicates
cursorform	graphics	project
date	if	ptr_dword
deletefile	include	

(continued)

random	scr_attr	text
readchar	scr_char	time
readdevice	shiftwindow	trace
readint	shorttrace	trail
readln	sin	upper_lower
readterm	sound	window_attr
reference	sqrt	window_str
removewindow	storage	write
renamefile	str_char	writedevice
retract	str_int	writef
right	system	
save	tan	

Figure 3.1 Turbo Prolog reserved and restricted terms

This section elaborates on the built-in predicates, primarily those supported by Turbo Prolog. Some have particular impact on an architectual principle—for example, I/O, turtle graphics or windowing—and bear evaluating in context; in such cases, an ancillary discussion may be found in the appropriate section. For instance, the use of the predicate readdevice is abstracted in this section but also explored in context in Section 4, "Input/Output."

Syntax

A built-in predicate must be typed in lower-case characters. As with other Prolog atoms, a predicate beginning with an initial capital letter will be interpreted as a variable name. Most, but not all, require an argument consisting of one or more object names. The objects have specific meanings based on position. For example, the Turbo Prolog predicate *makewindow* has the following format:

makewindow(1,7,7,"Suspected Organism,"3,0,16,54)

Each atom in the argument will be bound to a predefined variable. The first atom (1) will be interpreted as the window number, the fourth ("Suspected Organism") as the header, and the fifth (3) as the the beginning row number.

Technically, a predicate is a relation in a factual expression, but it does not necessarily require an argument. For example, *nl*, a standard predicate in all versions of Prolog, causes a new-line character—on an IBM PC, a carriage return—to be output. However, the same result may be produced with the write predicate, which outputs its argument:

```
write(' \ 13')
```

The single quotation marks indicate an object of the char domain, and the backslash denotes an ASCII equivalent. Hence, when Prolog executes this clause, it writes the equivalent of ASCII code 13, the carriage return.

append

Use:

In standard versions of Prolog, *append* combines the contents of two Prolog lists to create a third, all-inclusive list.

Format:

```
append(list1,list2,list3)
      where list1 =  first input list
            list2 =  second input list
            list3 =  output list
```

Examples:

```
append(Round1,Round2,Winners)
append([88,76],Scores,Composite)
append(X,Y,[A,K,Q,J,10])
```

Comments:

This common, "pure" Prolog predicate is not a built-in predicate in Turbo Prolog and must be defined by the user. In other versions of Prolog, the list-handling predicate *append* outputs a composite list derived from the contents of two designated lists. The predicate succeeds even if one of the source lists is empty. The argument consists of three objects; the first two represent the lists to be appended and the third refers to the output list.

The clause in the first example above combines the members of the list bound to *Round1* with those of *Round2* to create a composite list, *Winners*. The second example appends the list [88,76] to one bound by the variable *Scores*, and outputs the new list as *Composite*. The third example illustrates the use of *append* to define a relationship between three lists. If *X* and *Y* unbound, Prolog will attempt to find two lists whose contents, when appended, would result in the composite list [A,K,Q,J,10].

asserta

Use:

For evaluation before all other expressions with the corresponding predicate, *asserta* adds a clause to the top of the current database in RAM.

Examples:

```
asserta(workup(Test,Result))
asserta(X)
asserta(done(Process))
```

Comments:

The twin predicates *asserta* and *assertz* will both insert a new clause in the current database. The former is used to add the factual expression at the front, that is, before any other clauses constructed with the predicate in question.

Consider, for instance, the following fact:

```
asserta(attributes(Color,Meal)).
```

This clause might appear in an expert system designed to recommend a wine for any meal or occasion. Once the variables *Color* and *Meal* have been bound, a new clause—with *attributes* as its predicate and the bound values as its argument —will be inserted in the database before all other clauses containing the predicate *attributes*.

The "asserted" clause remains in the database indefinitely, or until a corresponding *retract* clause is evaluated. The predicate *retract* has the effect of removing a previously inserted clause from the database.

Figure 3.2 illustrates the use of *asserta* to extract data in an expert system. In the sample listing, a database is declared with the predicate attributes, stipulating three possible objects—*value*, *value*, and *meal*. The goal of the consultation is the program's recommendation, a subroutine constructed in the form of a compound rule. As it begins its pursuit, Turbo Prolog displays a window 25 rows by 80 columns with the header "Wine Consultant." The system then queries the operator to supply values for three variables—*X*, *Y*, and *Z*. The *asserta* clause adds a new clause to the database, using *attributes* as the predicate and the bound values of *X*, *Y*, and *Z* as the objects. Finding a match in the database, Turbo Prolog prints the variable bound in the conclusion.

```
domains
  value,meal  = symbol
  type        = string
database
  attributes(value,value,meal)
predicates
  wine(type)
  recommendation
  new_data
goal
  recommendation.
clauses
  wine("Cabernet Sauvignon"):-
        attributes(dry,red,beef).
  wine("Burgundy"):-
        attributes(dry,red,fish).
  wine("White Zinfandel"):-
        attributes(dry,white,beef).
  wine("Chenin Blanc"):-
        attributes(dry,white,fish).
  wine("Rose'"):-
        attributes(sweet,red,_).
  wine("Chablis"):-
        attributes(sweet,white,beef).
  wine("Reisling"):-
        attributes(sweet,white,fish).
  recommendation:-
        makewindow(1,7,7,"Wine Consultant",0,0,25,80),
        write("Do you prefer dry or sweet? "),
        readln(X),
        write("Do you prefer red or white? "),
        readln(Y),
        write("Is the meal beef or fish? "),
        readln(Z),
        asserta(attributes(X,Y,Z)),
        wine(W),nl,
        write("I recommend ",W),nl,nl,nl,nl,nl,
        new_data.
  new_data:-
        retract(attributes(_,_,_)),
        fail.
```

Figure 3.2 Using asserta to extract data

In MicroProlog, which runs on CP/M-based systems, the predicate ADDCL is used to add new clauses to the database.

Hazards:

A variable appearing in the argument must be bound to a syntactically correct clause. The maximum length of a bound variable in Turbo Prolog is 64 characters.

A clause added with asserta remains in the database even after backtracking. A *retract* clause must be used in the listing to prevent redundant evaluation.

References:

assertz; retract

assertz

Use:

For evaluation after all other clauses constructed with the corresponding predicate, *assertz* adds a clause at the bottom of the current database in RAM.

Examples:

```
assertz(Y)
assertz(part(Number))
assertz(valid(Object,Value))
```

Comments:

Both *asserta* and *assertz* will add a new clause to the current database. But *asserta* places the expression at the front of the database, and *assertz* places it at the end. Hence, the new fact will be evaluated only after all other clauses with the same predicate have been evaluated.

In Turbo Prolog, the database must be declared in the listing. Figure 3.3 illustrates the use of *assertz* in Turbo Prolog to extract data in an expert system. In the example, the goal of the consultation is a diagnosis producing the name of a suspected organism based on various clinical findings. The system begins its pursuit by drawing a window 25 rows by 80 columns with the header "Suspected Organism." The rules in the system contain the organism name in the conclusion and an object-value couplet in the premise. The operator is queried with close-ended questions requiring a yes or no response. Turbo Prolog evaluates each entry and sets a pointer to *t* or *f* for the corresponding fact based on whether the object-value couplet is true or false. The pointers determine the decision path until one of the conclusions can be confirmed, in which case the program outputs the name of the organism. If none of the conclusions can be supported, the phrase "Insufficient data" is output.

```
domains
  object,value,name = string
  choice            = symbol
database
  valid(object,value)
  invalid(object,value)
predicates
  diagnosis
  organism(name)
  true(object,value)
  query(object,value,choice)
  false(object,value)
  pointer(object,value,choice)
  new
goal
  diagnosis.
clauses
  diagnosis:-
        makewindow(1,7,7,"Suspected Organism",0,0,25,80),
        organism(Object),!,
        write("I suspect the organism is ",Object,". n"),
        nl,
        new.
  diagnosis:-
        write("Insufficient data."),
        nl,
        new.
  organism("Pseudomonas aeruginosa"):-
        true("the site of the infection","the blood") and
                true("the gram stain","positive") and
        true("the morphology of the organism","a rod")
                and true("the patient","feverish").
  organism("Staphyloccus aureus"):-
      ' true("the site of the infection",
                "the respiratory tract") and
        true("the leukocyte count","above 15,000") and
        true("the patient","prostate"),
        true("tachycardia","present").
  query(Object,Value,t):-
        write("Is ",Object," ",Value,"?"," n"),
        readln(Entry),
        frontchar(Entry,'y',_),!,
        pointer(Object,Value,t).
```

(continued)

```
query(Object,Value,f):-
     write("Is ",Object," ",Value,"?"," n"),
     readln(Entry),
     frontchar(Entry,'n',_),!,
     pointer(Object,Value,f).
     pointer(Object,Value,t):-
          assertz(valid(Object,Value)).
     pointer(Object,Value,f):-
          assertz(invalid(Object,Value)).
     true(Object,Value) if
          valid(Object,Value),!.


     true(Object,Value) if
          not(invalid(Object,Value)) and
                    query(Object,Value,t).
     false(Object,Value) if
          invalid(Object,Value),!.
     false(Object,Value) if
          not(valid(Object,Value)) and
                    query(Object,Value,f).
     new:-
          retract(valid(_,_)),
                    fail.
     new:-
          retract(invalid(_,_)),
                    fail.
```

Figure 3.3 Using *assertz* to extract data

In MicroProlog, which runs on CP/M-based systems, the predicate ADDCL is used to add new clauses to the database.

Hazards:

A variable appearing in the argument must be bound to a syntactically correct clause. The maximum length of a bound variable in Turbo Prolog is 64 characters.

A clause added with *asserta* remains in the database even after backtracking. A *retract* clause must be used in the listing to prevent redundant evaluation.

References:

asserta; retract

attribute

Use:

This predicate establishes a default video attribute for the entire display or reads the current video attribute.

Examples:

```
attribute(0)
attribute(23)
attribute(X)
```

Comments:

The *attribute* predicate is unique to Turbo Prolog and designed specifically to take advantage of the enhanced video display characteristics supported by the IBM PC. The argument must consist of an integer, or a variable bound to an integer, corresponding to an IBM PC monochrome or color/graphics display attribute.

Figure 3.4 gives several examples of monochrome and color graphics attribute values. A color graphics attribute value is actually the sum of two values: the value of the background color plus the value of the foreground color. Consult Figure 5.4 in Section 5 for a list of video attribute values, including both foreground and background colors.

If the argument is unbound, *attribute* reads the current video attribute.

Background	Foreground	Monitor Type	Value
Black	Black	Color/Monochrome	0
Black	Blue	Color	1
Black	Green	Color	2
Black	White	Color/Monochrome	7
Blue	Red	Color	20
Blue	White	Color	23
Green	Blue	Color	33
Green	White	Color	39
Magenta	Black	Color	80
Magenta	White	Color	87
Yellow	Red	Color	108
White	Black	Monochrome	112
Yellow	Green	Color	116
White	White	Color	119

Figure 3.4 Examples of IBM PC video attribute values in Turbo Prolog

back

Use:

This predicate moves the graphics turtle a stipulated number of points in the opposite direction of its most recent motion.

Examples:

```
back(1000)
back(X)
```

Comments:

The *back* predicate is a Turtle Graphics command supported by Turbo Prolog and used to reverse the direction of the pen, or turtle. Each point, or step, represents 1/32,000 of the horizontal or vertical dimension of the display.

The clause:

```
back(8000)
```

moves the turtle in the opposite direction of its most current motion by 8000 steps, or about one fourth the vertical or horizontal dimension of the screen. In the clause:

```
back(X)
```

X must be bound to an integer representing the desired number of steps.

Hazards:

The argument must consist of an integer smaller than the difference between 32,000 and the current position of the turtle. If the integer exceeds the number of points between the turtle and the edge of the display, the clause fails, with no visible effects on the pen.

beep

Use:

The *beep* predicate toots the PC's horn.

Examples:

beep

Comments:

As you might have guessed, the Turbo Prolog predicate *beep* is the IBM PC's equivalent of the console bell sound. The clause succeeds by outputting a tone to the computer's audio synthesizer. The same result can be produced with the I/O predicate *sound* but with the added flexibility of varying the pitch. For instance, to emit a high-pitched beep, use a high frequency:

sound(20,2000)

For a low-pitched beep, use a lower frequency, for example, 200.

References:

sound

bios

Use:

The *bios* predicate invokes a BIOS interrupt at stipulated registers.

Examples:

bios(33,reg(AX,0,0,DX,0,0,DS,0),_).
bios(33,reg(AX,0,0,0,0,0,0,0),reg(VV,_,_,_,_,_,_)).

Comments:

The argument consists of the interrupt number, input registers, and output registers. Each register is referenced as an argument consisting of the following special-purpose objects:

AX,BX,CX,DX,SI,DI,DS,ES

Each object name represents one of the 8086 processor's addressable registers. The subclause containing the input registers is entered first, followed by the subclause for the output registers.

bound

Use:

This predicate verifies variable binding in Turbo Prolog.

Examples:

```
bound(X)
bound(Organism)
```

Comments:

The Turbo Prolog predicate *bound* fails unless the variable named in the argument has previously been bound. It has the opposite effect of *free*, which succeeds only if the named variable has not been bound.

In standard versions of Prolog, the predicates *var* and *nonvar* are used to confirm variable binding, or *instantiation*.

References:

free

char_int

Use:

In Turbo Prolog, *char_int* converts an ASCII character to its decimal equivalent, or vica versa.

Examples:

```
char_int('a',X)
char_int(X,65)
char_int(X,Y)
```

Comments:

The Turbo Prolog predicate *char_int* converts keyboard characters to ASCII decimals or converts decimals to ASCII characters. The argument must contain first the character, or a variable corresponding to a character, followed by the decimal value, or a corresponding variable.

In the clause:

```
char_int('A',Y)
```

the variable *Y* will be bound to ASCII decimal 65. If only the decimal value in the argument is bound, as in the clause:

```
char_int(X,97)
```

the ASCII character will be returned. In this example, *X* will be bound to the character a.

In the following clause, *char_int* is used to compare a character and integer, both bound to variables:

```
char_int(X,Y)
```

The clause succeeds only if the decimal bound to *Y* is the ASCII equivalent of the character bound to *X*.

Hazards:

The documentation for Turbo Prolog 1.0 erroneously refers to this predicate as *char_ascii* in at least one place. The correct predicate name is *char_int*. In version 1.1, the correct name is given in an addendum.

References:

str_int; str_real

clearwindow

Use:

The *clearwindow* predicate erases the contents of the currently active window.

Examples:

```
clearwindow
```

Comments:

This predicate is one of Turbo Prolog's elegant window-handling facilities. The clause succeeds by changing the video attributes of all displayed characters inside the current window to the same attributes as the background. The effect is a clear screen affecting only the most recently activated window.

References:

makewindow; shiftwindow; window_attr

closefile

Use:

In Turbo Prolog, *closefile* closes a file by its symbolic filename, or synonym.

Examples:

```
closefile(rules)
closefile(X)
```

Comments:

The Turbo Prolog predicate *closefile* performs a normal file closure in an input/output routine. The argument consists of the symbolic filename by which the file was opened or a variable corresponding to the symbolic filename. The clause should be used following an *openappend, openmodify, openread,* or *openwrite* operation to allow the file to be reopened in the future.

References:

openappend; openmodify; openread; openwrite

comline

Use:

In Turbo Prolog 1.1, *comline* determines the command line used to execute a program from within the program.

Examples:

comline(L)

Comments:

Use *comline* to read the directory path or other parameters entered at the command line to execute the program. The argument consists of a variable which will be bound to the command line.

References:

system

concat

Use:

In Turbo Prolog, *concat* concatenates two strings and outputs the result as a third string, or it tests for concatenation between two strings.

Format:

concat(string1,string2,string3)
    where string1 = first input string
        string2 = second input string
        string3 = output string

Examples:

concat ("Smith","Albert",X)
concat(X,Y,Z)

Comments:

Use *concat* to concatenate two strings or to determine if two strings, if concatenated, are equivalent to a third string. The argument consists of three objects, the first pair representing input strings and the third corresponding to the concatenated output string. In the first example, the value of X is necessarily "Smith Albert." In the second example, if X and Y are known, their concatenated string would be bound to Z. Conversely, if all the variables are known, the goal fails unless the concatenation of X and Y is equivalent to the string bound to Z.

config

Use:

In Turbo Prolog 1.1, *config* loads a user-created configuration file within a program.

Examples:

```
config("screen.con")
```

Comments:

This predicate reads a designated file into memory for configuring the screen. Typical contents of the configuration file might include a default graphics mode, video attributes, and window specifications. The argument consists of the filename containing the configuration data.

References:

consult

consult

Use:

This predicate reads the contents of a disk file into the Prolog database.

Examples:

```
consult(X)
consult("test.dat")
```

Comments:

The Prolog predicate *consult* supplements the program listing with the entire contents of a file in storage. The clauses contained in the text file are evaluated as normal factual expressions.

The argument consists of the filename whose syntax depends on the Prolog version and operating system. In Turbo Prolog, the DOS filename or a variable bound to a DOS filename must be used. Note that a filename is technically a string and therefore should be enclosed in double quotation marks. In DEC prolog, the pathname or logical storage unit may be included in the filename.

Figure 3.5 illustrates the use of *consult* in a simple filing program. The file is constructed as a declared database, whose argument contains the record fields. Turbo Prolog pursues the goal by consulting the DOS file employee.dat, stored in the current directory. In this example, the text file might contain the following clauses:

```
employee("Sawyer","520-12-9123","Maintenance",1500).
employee("Thatcher","562-09-7220","Drafting",2500).
employee("Finn","532-66-1822","Engineering",3500).
```

```
domains
  last_name,soc_sec_no,department          = string
  salary                                   = integer
database
  employee(last_name,soc_sec_no,department,salary)
predicates
  get_salary
goal
  consult("employee.dat"),
  get_salary.
clauses
  get_salary:-
        write("Last name? "),
        readln(X),
        employee(X,_,_,Y),
        write(X,"'s salary is ",Y),
        keypressed.
```

Figure 3.5 Using consult in a simple filing program

When all the clauses have been read into the RAM database, the operator is prompted for a retrieval key, in this case, the employee's last name. Turbo Prolog reads the entry (*X*) and binds it to the object last_name. Finding a match in the database, the system outputs the value of *Y*, which is bound to salary. For instance:

Thatcher's salary is 2500

Hazards:

When the listing containing the *consult* predicate is compiled, no check is performed on the syntax of the facts contained in the named file. If any errors are encountered among the stored clauses on execution, the predicate fails and the decision tree is aborted.

The following restrictions apply to the contents of a consulted file:

- Any symbols in the file will be stored as strings; hence, any objects of the symbol domain must begin and end with double quotation marks. No blank lines are allowed in the file.

- If an unbound variable or invalid filename is used in the argument, the clause will also fail. In Turbo Prolog, a filename not enclosed in double quotation marks is invalid.

cursor

Use:

In Turbo Prolog, cursor positions the cursor at a specified row and column or retrieves the current cursor position.

Format:

```
cursor(row,column)
```

Examples:

```
cursor(0,0)
cursor(12,8)
cursor(X,10)
```

Comments:

The argument consists of the row and column where the cursor is to be positioned or variables corresponding to the row or column. The values, either actual or bound, must be integers. The first integer in the argument will always be interpreted as the row number and the second as the column number.

When the clause:

```
cursor(0,0)
```

is encountered, the cursor will be positioned at the home position (row 0, column 0). In the clause:

```
cursor(10,Y)
```

the cursor position is defined as row 10 at the column value to which the variable *Y* is bound. If *Y* is unbound, the current column number will be returned. Similary, the clause:

```
cursor(X,5)
```

will place the cursor at column 5 in the row whose value is bound to *X*. If *X* has not previously been instantiated, the current row value will be returned.

Variables may also be used for both objects in the argument, as in the clause:

```
cursor(R,C)
```

If both variables are unbound, the row and column of the current cursor positions will be returned.

Hazards:

Only integers may be used to designate row and column positions. Hence, for the predicate to succeed, the value bound to a variable for the row or column must be an integer. Rounding off may be required if the variable is determined by a calculation in which a fraction or dividend is possible.

A window is treated internally as a separate console; that is, the row and column numbers are relative within the active window. Hence, row 0, column 0 represents the home position of the current window even though the window itself may begin at row 12, column 40, for example.

References:

cursorform

cursorform

Use:

In Turbo Prolog, *cursorform* adjusts the cursor height from 1 to 14 scanlines.

Format:

cursorform(bottom,top)

Examples:

cursorform(1,14)
cursorform(5,10)
cursorform(1,X)

Comments:

The argument consists of two integers, the first representing the scanline at the bottom of the cursor and the second denoting the scanline at the top. The minimum value for the bottom scanline is 1 and the maximum value for the top is 14. Hence, the second integer must be larger than the first.

The clause in the first example extends the cursor to full block mode, that is, to its maximum height of 14 scanlines. The second example forms a hyphen-like cursor beginning 5 scanlines up from the base of a formed character and extending an additional 6 scanlines. In the third example, the height is bound to the variable *X*.

date

Use:

In Turbo Prolog, *date* retrieves the current system date on output or establishes a new system date on input.

Format:

date(year,month,day)

Examples:

```
date(87,10,04)
date(X,Y,Z)
```

Comments:

The argument consists of three integers, each representing a date component. The first object will always be interpreted as the last two digits of the year and the second as the numeric month code. The clause in the first example sets the computer's internal clock to 84/10/07 (October 7, 1984). The second example retrieves the current date from the PC's clock, binding the year to *X*, the month to *Y*, and the day to *Z*.

deletefile

Use:

In Turbo Prolog, *deletefile* permits a specified file to be deleted from storage within a program.

Format:

```
deletefile(filename.ext)
```

Examples:

```
deletefile("scratch.fil")
deletefile(X)
```

Comments:

The argument consists of the DOS filename for the file to be deleted. The specified file must reside in the current storage area, that is, the currently logged disk and directory.

References:

existfile; renamefile

dir

Use:

In Turbo Prolog, *dir* enables a specified disk directory to be displayed or searched within a program.

Format:

    dir(Disk/Directory,Filespec,Filename)

Examples:

    dir(" \ prolog"," *.pro",Commodity)
    dir(" \ employee \ data"," *.dat",_)
    dir(X," *.*",_)
    dir(" \ storage",X,Y)

Comments:

The argument consists of three objects, the first representing the directory name, the second indicating the file specification, and the third constituting a free variable to be bound to a filename selected with a carriage return. The directory name specifies the path. When determinate names are used, they must be enclosed in double quotation marks.

The clause:

    dir(" \ \ prolog"," *.pro",Commodity)

will display the directory of \ *prolog* for the files described by the wildcard filename *.pro*. When an anonymous variable is used for the filename, as in the clause:

    dir(" \ prolog"," *.pro",_)

the returned value for the filename will be ignored. When variables are used in the argument, they must be bound to strings designating the desired directory path and file specification.

Hazards:

The filename cannot be bound; an error message will result on compilation.

References:

disk; existfile

disk

Use:

In Turbo Prolog, *disk* changes the currently logged disk and specifies a directory path or retrieves the current path.

Format:

disk(" drive letter \ path")

Examples:

disk(" a: \ \ prolog")
disk(X)

Comments:

The argument consists of the drive letter and DOS directory path enclosed in double quotation marks, or a corresponding variable. Figure 3.6 illustrates a sample routine incorporating the Turbo Prolog predicates *disk* and *dir*.

```
get_disk:-

        makewindow(1,7,7,"Disk",0,0,14,24),

        write("Disk\directory path: "),

        readln(X),

        disk(X),

        dir(X,"*.pro",_).
```

Figure 3.6 Routine incorporating disk and dir

The sample routine creates a directory window of 14 rows by 24 columns and then prompts the operator for the disk letter and directory path. The response (*X*) is bound to the drive path in both the disk clause and the dir clause. Turbo Prolog changes the default drive to the input value for *X*, then displays the directory of all files with the extension .pro in the window.

If the argument is unbound, *disk* will return the current path.

display

Use:

In Turbo Prolog, *display* outputs or retrieves a specified string on the screen.

Examples:

```
display(Employee)
display("Please stand by")
display(X)
```

Comments:

The argument consists of the string or a variable bound to the specified string. The string will be displayed in the currently active window. If the string is larger than the available character positions inside the window, the cursor keys may be used to scroll the display.

Note: Display is normally used with *file_str* to display large text files.

References:

edit; window_str; file_str

dot

Use:

In conjunction with the *graphics* predicate, *dot* paints a dot at a specified row and column or reads the color at a specified row and column.

Format:

```
dot(row,column,color)
```

Examples:

```
dot(1000,16000,2)
dot(X,Y,3)
dot(R,C,X)
```

Comments:

The argument consists of three object names, the first representing the row number, the second the column number, and the third the dot color. The screen must previously have been initialized with a *graphics* clause designating the mode, palette, and background color. Available colors for the Turbo Prolog palettes specified by the *graphics* predicate are shown in Figure 3.7.

Dot Color	Graphics Palettte	Screen Color
1	0	Green
1	1	Cyan
2	0	Red
2	1	Magenta
3	0	Yellow
3	1	White

Figure 3.7 Turbo Prolog palette colors

Assume, for instance, that the following clause is used to set up a graphics display:

```
graphics(1,0,1)
```

The first two objects in the argument represent the graphics mode and the palette selection. In this clause, the mode is 1 (medium resolution) and the palette selection is 0. Hence, the following clause would paint a red dot in the center of the screen:

```
dot(16000,16000,2)
```

Note that the row and column values are independent of the row and column dimensions of the selected display mode. Turbo Prolog considers each point on the screen to represent 1/32,000 of the verical or horizontal dimension. Hence, the center is always row 16,000, column 16,000, regardless of the screen resolution.

The predicate *dot* may also be used to determine the current color by using a variable in place of the color value.

edit

Use:

In Turbo Prolog, *edit* enables a specified string to be edited by the built-in text editor and output as a second string.

Format:

edit(string1,string2)

Examples:

edit(Letter,New_letter)
edit(″Patient name″,Pname)
edit(″ ″,Document)

Comments:

The predicate *edit* invokes the built-in text editor and loads the specified input string (string1) into the most recently referenced window. The effect is to transform the current window into a full-function text editor supporting WordStar®-like commands and conventions. When the edited string is saved, the modified contents are output as a second string (string2).

The clause in the first example loads a string bound to the variable Letter for editing, and then it saves the edited text as the output string New letter. The second example loads the string "*Patient name*" into the editor for output as a string bound to the variable *pname*. In the third example, a blank string will be edited, permitting the creation of new text.

Figure 3.8 demonstrates the use of the *edit* predicate to create an internal screen editor in a Turbo Prolog application.

When the goal *create* is pursued, a window frame outlines the entire screen with the header "Screen Editor" in the top crossbar. The operator is prompted for the variable *N*, which represents the filename by which the edited text will be saved. The built-in editor is invoked with a blank string with the output bound to the variable Text. The operator uses WordStar-like commands to create and edit the string. When the session is terminated with an F10 key press, a DOS file is opened for writing, using the user-defined DOS filename bound to *N*, and the string is written into it.

```
domains

    file = document

predicates

    create

clauses

    create:-

        makewindow(1,7,7,"Screen Editor",0,0,25,80),

        write("File Name: "), readln(N),

        edit("",Text),

        openwrite(document,N),

        writedevice(document),

        write(Text).
```

Figure 3.8 Using edit to create an internal screen editor

Figure 3.9 lists sample editing commands supported by the built-in editor.

Function	Command
Toggle insert mode	Ctrl-V
Delete character right	Ctrl-G
Delete character left	Del
Delete word right	Ctrl-T
Delete current line	Ctrl-Y
Mark beginning of block	Ctrl-KB
Mark end of block	Ctrl-KK
Copy block	Ctrl-KC
Move block	Ctrl-KV
Delete block	Ctrl-KY
Search and replace	Ctrl-QA
Find string	Ctrl-QF
Quit	F10

Figure 3.9 Sample Turbo Prolog editing commands

References:

editmsg

editmsg

Use:

Turbo Prolog's built-in text editor is invoked with *editmsg*, and it enables a specified string to be edited for output as a second string. The active window display is enhanced by two headers, a user-defined message at the bottom, and a help facility.

Format:

```
editmsg(string1,string2,header1,header2,msg,help,pos,code)
     where      string1 = input string
                string2 = output string
                header1 = left header
                header2 = right header
                msg     = user-defined message
                help    = user-created help file
                pos     = cursor position
                code    = 1 or 0
```

Examples:

```
editmsg(Label,Smith_label,"Mail List","Edit Mode","Press F10
     to Save",Helpmail,15,X)
```

Comments:

Like *edit*, this predicate invokes the built-in text editor, which supports WordStar-like commands and conventions and loads the specified input string (string1). Two headers are displayed at the top of the window, and a message of the programmer's own device is displayed at the bottom. In addition, a custom help file may be specified for access with the PC's F1 function key. The fifth object represents the name of the help file. The sixth object in the argument specifies the cursor position in the input string. The final object represents a code (either 1 or 0) to indicate the method by which the editor was last terminated (by pressing either F10 or ESC, respectively).

References:

edit

eof

Use:

In Turbo Prolog, *eof* monitors a specified file for the end-of-file marker.

Examples:

```
eof(Scr1)
eof(input)
not(eof(X))
```

Comments:

The argument consists of the symbolic name, or synonym, of the file to be monitored. The predicate succeeds when the current place in a file is the end-of-file marker. Hence, the compound predicate *not(eof(X))* enables a process to be repeated until the end-of-file marker is reached.

Figure 3.10 illustrates the use of *eof* and *not(eof* in an input/output routine.

```
domains
    type,color,vineyard    = string
    vintage                = integer
    file                   = inventory
    item                   = stock(type,vintage,color,vineyard)

predicates
    wine
    search_inventory(file)

goal
    wine.

clauses
    wine:-
        makewindow(1,7,7,"Wine Cellar",0,0,15,30),
        write("Color: "),
        readln(Color),
        openread(inventory,"current.dat"),
        readdevice(inventory),
        search_inventory(inventory),
        readterm(item,stock(Type,Vintage,Color,Vineyard)),
        nl,nl,
        write("Name      : ",Type),nl,
        write("Vintage   : ",Vintage),nl,
        write("Vineyard  : ",Vineyard),nl,
        keypressed.
    search_inventory(_).
    search_inventory(C):-
        not(eof(C)),
        search_inventory(C).
```

Figure 3.10 Using eof and not(eof in an input/output routine

References:

not; openappend; openread; openwrite; readdevice

existfile

Use:

Searches the currently logged storage unit for a specified file.

Examples:

```
existfile("smith.rec")
existfile(S)
```

Comments:

The argument consists of the DOS filename enclosed in double quotation marks for the desired file or, alternatively, an instantiated variable bound to a DOS filename. The predicate *existfile* searches the currently logged disk and directory. If a different disk or directory is to be searched, a disk clause must have previously been used to change the default drive and directory path.

References:

disk; dir

exit

Use:

The *exit* predicate terminates the program and returns to the system (either Prolog or DOS).

Comments:

In Turbo Prolog, the predicate *exit* succeeds by halting execution of the program or module currently in progress and returning to the system. If the program was executed as a compiled, linked EXE file, control will be returned to DOS; if the program was executed from the Turbo menu system, control will be returned to the command menu. In other versions of Prolog, *exit* halts the processing of clauses and returns the operator to the conversational mode.

fail

Use:

Enforces backtracking at the point of insertion.

Examples:

```
new_data:-
        retract(attributes(_,_,_)),
        fail.

list:_
     suspected(Organism),
     write(Organism),
     fail.

find:-
        disk(c:" \ evidence"),
        existfile("wt1033.doc"),!,
        fail.
```

Comments:

The Prolog predicate *fail* always fails. The effect is to initiate backtracking at the point of insertion. The three examples illustrate various routines expressed as compound goals. In the first routine, a *retract* clause is used to remove the first previously asserted clause from the database. Here, *fail* is used to force backtracking, until no more clauses can be found for removal. In the second example, *fail* is used to list all possible solutions to the clause *suspected(organism)*; and in the third example, a conjunction with the cut atom (!) causes the entire goal to fail, preventing further pursuit.

field_attr

Use:

This predicate establishes or changes the video attributes of a specified field or returns the attribute if the attribute variable is unbound.

Format:

```
field_attr(row,col,len,attr)
      where row =  beginning row number
            col =  beginning column number
            len =  length of field
            attr = attribute value
```

Examples:

```
field_attr(2,2,32,112)
field_attr(8,10,24,Y)
```

Comments:

The Turbo Prolog predicate *field_attr* enables the programmer to alter the screen attribute of a field positioned in a previously defined window. The length of the field must not be greater than the size of the current window. The argument consists of four objects: the first representing the row number, the second the column number, the third the field length, and the fourth the corresponding value for the desired video attribute.

The clause in the first example sets the field at row 2, column 2 of the active window to inverse video; the specified field length is 32 characters. In the second example, the current field attribute will be bound to the variable *Y*.

The attribute value is determined by the desired foreground and background colors for the field in question. Figure 3.4 illustrates several sample values. The method of computing attribute values for Turbo Prolog's screen-handling predicates is discussed in Section 5.

Hazards:

The row and column numbers used in this predicate are relative to the dimensions and placement of the most recently referenced window. For instance, row 2, column 10 in a window, relative to the monitor screen, might actually be something like row 13, column 41. Bear in mind that the outline, or frame, of the window occupies the outermost row and column. Hence, the home position inside a window is actually row 1, column 1, not row 0, column 0.

References:

attribute; window_attr; makewindow; shiftwindow

field_str

Use:

In Turbo Prolog, *field_str* loads a specified string into a displayed field or reads the contents of a displayed field.

Format:

```
field_str(row,col,len,str)
        where row = beginning row number
              col = beginning column number
              len = length of field
              str = string
```

Examples:

```
field_str(4,2,56,Patient)
field_str(12,8,28," ")
```

Comments:

The Turbo Prolog predicate *field_str* places a specified string in a field positioned in a previously defined window. The argument consists of four objects: the first representing the row number where the field begins; the second, the beginning column number; the third designating the field length; and the fourth representing the desired string, or, typically, the variable bound to the string. The row and column numbers are relative to the active window. If the string length is greater than the field length, only the number of characters specified in the argument will be displayed. However, the field length must be smaller than the number of characters provided by the most recently referenced window.

Hazards:

The row and column numbers used in this predicate are relative to the dimensions and placement of the most recently referenced window. For instance, row 2, column 10 in a window, relative to the monitor screen, might actually be something like row 13, column 41. Bear in mind that the outline, or frame, of the window occupies the outermost row and column. Hence, the home position inside a window is actually row 1, column 1, not row 0, column 0.

filemode

Use:

In Turbo Prolog 1.1, *filemode* accesses a binary file by its symbolic name, or synonym.

Format:

```
filemode(synonym, mode)
        where synonym  =  symbolic name
               mode    =  0 or 1
```

Examples:

```
filemode(binfile,1)
filemode(textfile,0)
```

Comments:

Use *filemode* to access a binary file in either text mode or binary mode. The argument consists of the symbolic name (synonym) for the binary file, followed by 0 (text mode) or 0 (binary mode).

filepos

Use:

The predicate *filepos* specifies the file position for writing to the file.

Format:

```
filepos(file,pos,mode)
        where file   = symbolic name
               pos    = position
               mode   = file mode value
```

Examples:

```
filepos(datafile,P,2)
```

Comments:

The Turbo Predicate *filepos* is used in input/output to determine the point at which new data will be written to a file in memory. The argument consists of three objects: the first designating the symbolic name, or synonym, of the file to be written to; the second representing the file position; and the third, a value corresponding to one of three possible file modes. The clause in the example determines the file position (P) relative to the end of the file in a datafile currently open for writing.

Figure 3.11 illustrates the use of *filepos* in a file write operation. In this routine, as in the example, the file position is determined in relation to the end of the file. The three Turbo Prolog file modes are interpreted as follows.

Mode	Relation
0	Beginning of file
1	Current position
2	End of file

```
domains
      file        = datafile

predicates
      add_rec(dbasedom,string)

clauses
      add_rec(Data,Records):-
            openappend(datafile,Records),
            writedevice(datafile),
            filepos(datafile,P,2),
            write(Data,\nl),
            closefile(datafile).
```

Figure 3.11 Example use of the Turbo Prolog predicate filepos

References:

write

file_str

Use:

In Turbo Prolog, *file_str* loads the contents of a file from storage into a specified string.

Format:

file_str(filename,String)

Examples:

file_str("elmirage.dsc",S1)

Comments:

This predicate is used to extract data from a file in storage for string manipulation in RAM. Typical applications include retrieving disk data for display, editing, or type conversion. The clause in the example converts the contents of the disk file *elmirage.dsc* to a string, bound to the variable S1.

The argument consists of two objects: the first specifying the disk file by its DOS filename and the second naming the variable by which the string will be referenced.

Hazards:

This predicate specifies a file on the default disk and directory. It may be necessary to precede a *file_str* clause with a disk clause to change the currently logged storage area. For example:

```
get_string:-
        disk("a:\ morphol"),
        file_str("staph.aur",Morphology).
```

The predicate *file_str* will only read a file up to 64K in size.

findall

Use:

This predicate creates a list of all the values bound to a variable in a specified predicate.

Format:

```
findall(Var,pred,List)
        where Var   = variable to be listed
              pred  = corresponding predicate
              List  = list reference
```

Examples:

findall(Organism,suspected(Organism),Suspects)

Comments:

The Prolog predicate *findall* compiles a list of all the solutions that satisfy a given predicate as a result of backtracking. The argument consists of three objects: the first representing the variable, the second the predicate, and the third a variable by which the output list will be referenced. The clause in the example finds all the values bound to the variable *Organism* in the clause:

suspected(Organism)

and outputs the results in the form of a Prolog list bound to the variable *Suspects*. If no values have been bound to the specified variable, the contents of the output list will be *nil*.

References:

bound; free; append

flush

Use:

This predicate flushes the file buffer by sending the contents to the most recently referenced list device.

Examples:

flush(datafile)

flush(input)

Comments:

The Turbo Prolog predicate *flush* is used to empty the contents of the file buffer to the peripheral corresponding to the last writedevice clause. The device may be a predefined Turbo Prolog file, for example, *printer*, or it may be a user-defined file referring to a peripheral or port. The argument consists of the symbolic name, or synonym, for the designated device.

References:

writedevice

forward

Use:

This predicate moves the graphics turtle a stipulated number of points in the current direction of its most recent motion.

Examples:

```
forward(720)
forward(Y)
```

Comments:

The *forward* predicate is a Turtle Graphics command supported by Turbo Prolog and used to advance the pen, or turtle. Each point, or step, represents 1/32,000 of the horizontal or vertical dimension of the display.

Hazards:

The argument must consist of an integer smaller than the difference between 32,000 and the current position of the turtle. If the integer exceeds the number of points between the turtle and the edge of the display, the clause fails with no visible effects on the pen.

free

Use:

The predicate *free* verifies that a variable is unbound in Turbo Prolog.

Examples:

```
free(X)
free(Commodity)
```

Comments:

The predicate *free* always fails unless the stipulated variable has not been bound to a value. It has the opposite effect of *bound*, which succeeds only if the named variable has been bound.

References:

bound

---

frontchar

Use:

The predicate *frontchar* acts on a designated string to separate the front character from the remaining characters.

Format:

```
frontchar(Str,Front,Etc)
       where  Str  = string to be separated
              Front = front character
              Etc  = remaining characters
```

Examples:

```
frontchar(Entry,X,Y)
frontchar(Choice,'y',_)
```

Comments:

The Turbo Prolog predicate *frontchar* concatenates the initial character in a string with the remaining characters. The effect is to separate the front character. The argument consists of three objects: the first referencing the string, the second representing the front character, and the third representing the remaining characters in the string.

In the first example if *Entry* were bound to an existing string, its front character would be bound to X and the trailing characters would be bound to Y. Conversely, if X and Y were bound, their respective characters would be concatenated into the string *Entry*.

The clause in the second example tests the string Choice to determine if the first character is the letter y.

Hazards:

Either the variable corresponding to the string must previously have been bound, or the variables for the front character and remaining string must both have been bound. An anonymous variable (_) may only be used in deference to the front character or the trailing characters.

If the initial character(s) in a string is a Prolog token (e.g., an integer, sign, or predicate), *fronttoken* must be used to separate the token.

References:

frontstr;fronttoken

frontstr

Use:

This predicate separates a designated string into two different strings.

Format:

```
frontstr(char,Source,Target1,Target2)
        where char   = number of characters
              Source  = source string
              Target1 = first target string
              Target2 = second target string
```

Examples:

```
frontstr(4,Entry,X,Y)
frontstr(Z,Value,Key,Tail)
```

Comments:

The Turbo Prolog predicate *frontstr* splits a string into two separate strings for handling. The argument consists of four objects: the first specifying the character position at which the division will occur; the second is the variable corresponding to the string to be split; the third names front string; and the fourth names the string which will contain the trailing characters. The front string will contain the number of characters specified at the beginning of the argument.

In the first example, the clause splits the string *Entry* into two new strings, *X* and *Y*, placing the first two characters in *X* and the remaining characters in *Y*. In the second example, the value of the character position is bound to the variable *Z*.

Hazards:

If the initial character(s) in a string is a Prolog token, (e.g., an integer, sign, or predicate), *fronttoken* must be used to separate the token.

References:

frontchar; fronttoken

fronttoken

Use:

The predicate *fronttoken* extracts a Prolog token from the beginning of a string.

Format:

```
fronttoken(String1,Token,String2)
       where String1 = source string
             Token   = extracted token
             String2 = target string containing the remainder
```

Examples:

```
fronttoken(Entry,X,Y)
fronttoken(Z,144,_)
```

Comments:

The Turbo Prolog predicate *fronttoken* splits a designated string with a token at the beginning, thereby extracting the token. The remainder of the string, less the token, is placed in a new string. The argument consists of three objects: the first specifies the string from which the token is to be extracted; the second represents the token; and the third corresponds to the string containing the trailing characters.

In the first example, if *Entry* were bound to an existing string, *X* and *Y* would subsequently be bound to the front token and trailing characters, respectively. Conversely, if *X* and *Y* were previously bound, their contents would be concatenated into the string *Entry*.

The second example checks the string *Z* to determine if the front token is the integer 144.

Hazards:

Either the variable corresponding to the source string must previously have been bound, or the variables for the token and trailing characters must both have been bound.

gotowindow

Use:

In Turbo Prolog 1.1, *gotowindow* transfers the cursor and all succeeding write operations to a designated window, without saving the contents of the current window.

Examples:

```
gotowindow(4)
gotowindow(X)
```

Comments:

The argument consists of the window number designated when the window was originally created with makewindow. This predicate has the effect of transferring the current dialog from one window to another, without having to save the string displayed in the current window or redisplay the former contents of the destination window.

References:

shiftwindow; makewindow; window_str; field_str

graphics

Use:

In Turbo Prolog, *graphics* selects a graphics mode for medium-, high-, or enhanced-resolution display.

Format:

graphics(mode,palette,background)

Examples:

graphics(4,0,3)

Comments:

The *graphics* predicate is specific to Turbo Prolog and designed to take advantage of the IBM PC's diverse graphics capabilities. The argument consists of three integers, representing, in order, the graphics mode, palette selection, and background color.

The example above initializes the screen for high-resolution color graphics (4) using the Turbo Prolog green-red-yellow palette (0) on a cyan background (3).

The graphics mode is an arbitrary value representing the screen resolution. It is a function, in part, of the type of display adaptor installed on the computer. Figure 3.12 lists the values for the Turbo Prolog graphics modes.

Mode	Display	Resolution	Value
CGA	Medium resolution 4 colors	200 × 320	1
CGA	High resolution monochrome	200 × 640	2
EGA	Medium resolution 16 colors	200 × 320	3
EGA	High resolution 16 colors	200 × 640	4
EGA	Enhanced 13 colors	350 × 640	5

Figure 3.12 Turbo Prolog graphics modes

The palette value may be either 1 (cyan-magenta-white) or 0 (green-red-yellow). The exact color used by the graphics pen is determined by a subsequent dot or pencolor clause.

The background color may be an integer from 0 to 15. Figure 3.13 lists the available colors with their respective values.

Mode	Background	Value
3,4,5	Black	0
3,4,5	Blue	1
3,4,5	Green	2
3,4,5	Cyan	3
3,4,5	Red	4
3,4,5	Magenta	5
3,4,5	Brown	6
1,2	Black	7
3,4,5	White	7
3,4,5	Gray	8
3,4,5	Light blue	9
3,4,5	Light green	10
3,4,5	Light cyan	11
3,4,5	Light red	12
3,4,5	Light magenta	13
3,4,5	Yellow	14
3,4,5	Intense white	15
1,2	White	112

Figure 3.13 Turbo Prolog background colors

isname

Use:

This predicate checks to see if a designated string is the same as a reserved or restricted Turbo Prolog name.

Examples:

    isname(X)

Comments:

The *isname* predicate fails if the specified string X is not a reserved or restricted name.

References:

fronttoken

left

Use:

The *left* predicate rotates the direction of the graphics turtle a specified number of degrees to the left.

Examples:

```
left(45)
left(A)
```

Comments:

In Turbo Prolog, *left* is used to change the direction of the pen, or turtle. The argument may consist of an integer representing the desired angle in degrees or a variable which will be bound to the current angle. If the angle is not bound, the current angle will be returned.

References:

right; back; forward

line

Use:

The *line* predicate draws a line on the graphics screen from one specified point to another.

Format:

```
line(row1,col1,row2,col2,color)
```

Examples:

```
line(1000,1000,1000,31000,3)
line(1000,1000,X,Y,Paint)
```

Comments:

The Turbo Prolog predicate *line* creates a solid line beginning at a specified row and column and terminating at another specified row and column. The color value depends on the palette and graphics mode. The argument consists of five objects: the first and second represent the beginning row and column number; the third and fourth designate the terminating point; and the final object is the color value.

A graphics mode must have been previously invoked with a *graphics* clause, selecting the screen resolution, palette, and background color. Figure 3.14 lists several sample color values available in graphics mode 1, the resolution supported by the IBM PC Color Graphics Adaptor.

Line Color	Graphics Palette	Screen Color
1	0	Green
1	1	Cyan
2	0	Red
2	1	Magenta
3	0	Yellow
3	1	White

Figure 3.14 Sample Turbo Prolog line colors

Assume, for instance, that the following clause has been used to initialize the display:

```
graphics(1,0,1)
```

The first two objects in the argument represent the graphics mode and the palette selection. In this clause, the mode is 1 (medium resolution) and the palette selection is 0. Hence, the following clause could be used to paint a solid red line from the point at row 31000, column 1000 to the point at row 1000, column 1000:

```
line(31000,1000,1000,1000,2)
```

Note that the row and column numbers are independent of the row and column dimensions of the selected display mode. Turbo Prolog considers each point on the screen to represent 1/32,000 of the vertical or horizontal dimension.

The predicate *line* may also be used to determine the current color by using a variable in place of the color value.

References:

dot

makewindow

Use:

The predicate *makewindow* creates a window of specified dimensions at a designated position on the screen.

Format:

```
makewindow(num,attr1,attr2,header,row,col,ht,wd)
    where num    = window number
          attr1  = background/foreground attribute
          attr2  = outline attribute
          header = window header
          row    = beginning row
          col    = beginning column
          ht     = height in rows
          wd     = width in columns
```

Examples:

```
makewindow(1,7,7,"Diagnostic Consultation",0,0,25,80)
makewindow(3,7,7,"Passenger Data",12,0,10,40)
```

Comments:

The Turbo Prolog predicate *makewindow* creates a custom window for the programmer's application. The argument specifies the video attributes, a header line or message to appear at the top, the screen position, and the dimensions. The first object is an integer representing the window number. The second and third objects are also integers, specifying the video attributes inside the window and the definition of the window itself. The fourth object in the argument is an optional text header or a variable bound to a string to be used as a header. If a header is named in the argument, the text must be enclosed in double quotation marks. The header may also be a variable bound to a string. The remaining atoms are all integers, defining the beginning row, beginning column, height in rows, and width in columns.

In the first example, the window (1) uses normal video (attribute 7). The foreground color of the outline, or window frame, is white (7). The header *"Diagnostic Consultation"* will be displayed at the top of the window in the center of the crossbar. The position of the upper right corner will be row 0, column 0 (the home position), and the overall size of the window will be 25 rows by 80 columns, that is, the entire monitor screen.

Inverse video may also be used in the window. If the frame attribute is set to 0, the outline and header will be omitted.

Figure 3.4 lists several examples of Turbo Prolog video attribute values.

References:

attribute; shiftwindow; window_attr; window_str; removewindow; gotowindow; clearwindow

membyte

Use:

The predicate *membyte* stores a given byte at a specified memory address and offset.

Format:

```
membyte(seg,off,byte)
        where seg = memory segment
              off  = offset
```

Examples:

```
membyte(X,Y,Byte1)
```

Comments:

The argument consists of three integers or variables whose bound values are integers. The first represents the memory segment where the byte is to be stored. The second integer represents the offset value, and the third represents the byte. If the variable referring to the byte has not been bound, the clause returns the value of the memory segment and offset.

References:

portbyte; memword

memword

Use:

The predicate *memword* stores the value of a word at a specified address and offset.

Format:

```
memword(seg,off,word)
        where seg = memory segment
              off = offset
```

Examples:

```
memword(X,Y,Word1)
```

Comments:

The argument consists of three integers, or variables whose bound values are integers. The first represents the memory segment where the word is to be stored. The second integer represents the offset value, and the third represents the word. If the variable referring to the word has not been bound, the clause returns the value of the memory segment and offset.

References:

membyte; ptr_dword

nl

Use:

The *nl* predicate transmits a new-line character, or carriage return, to the current output stream.

Comments:

The *nl* predicate has no argument. The clause succeeds by outputting the ASCII decimal code 13. Hence, the same effect can be produced in a write statement using either the atom \ *13* or \ *n* in the argument. Both of the following clause lines succeed with the same results:

```
write("What is the purpose of the consultation?"),nl,
write("What is the purpose of the consultation?,\13"),
```

Figure 3.15 illustrates the use of *nl* in a simple query routine.

```
ST_segment:-
     write("Is the S-T segment: "),nl,
     nl,
     write("  a. Inverted?"),nl,
     write("  b. Elevated?"),nl
     write("  c. Normal?"),nl,
     nl,
     readln(Choice).
```

Figure 3.15 Sample query routine with nl

not

Use:

The predicate *not* succeeds if the compound object in its argument fails.

Examples:

```
not(eof(datafile))
not(suspected(Organism))
```

Comments:

The argument normally consists of a compound object representing a subclause. The *not* clause succeeds as long as the subclause fails. When and if the subclause fails, *not* succeeds and backtracking is terminated. In the first example, the clause enforces backtracking until the end-of-file marker is found, that is, until the subclause *eof(datafile)* succeeds. In the second example, backtracking is enforced as soon as a value becomes bound to the variable *Organism*.

References:

free; bound; eof

openappend

Use:

This predicate opens a disk file for appending, using a symbolic name (synonym).

Format:

openappend(synonym,filename)

Examples:

openappend(datafile,"records.med")
openappend(datafile,"accounts.dat")

Comments:

In Turbo Prolog, *openappend* is used in a disk input/output operation to open a file for appending. This predicate is used when the accessed file contains existing records, and a *write* clause will be used to append the file. The argument consists of the symbolic filename (synonym) by which the file will be referenced, followed by the actual DOS filename.

If the file resides in a different storage area than the default disk and directory, a disk clause may be used to change the drive letter and directory path. To open a disk file for both reading and writing, the built-in predicate *openmodify* must be used.

Figure 3.16 illustrates the use of *openappend* in a disk write operation.

```
predicates
    add_data

clauses
    add_data:-
        openappend(datafile,"pharmac.dat"),
        writedevice(datafile),
        filepos(datafile,P,0),
        write(Data,'\n'),
        closefile(datafile).
```

Figure 3.16 Sample use of openappend in a disk write operation

References:

openmodify; openread; openwrite; writedevice; closefile

openmodify

Use:

The *openmodify* predicate opens a disk file for reading and writing, using a symbolic name (synonym).

Format:

openmodify(synonym,filename)

Examples:

openmodify(datafile,"records.med")
openmodify(datafile,"accounts.dat")

Comments:

The Turbo Prolog predicate *openmodify* is used in a disk input/output operation to open a file for both reading and writing. The argument consists of the symbolic filename (synonym) by which the file will be referenced, followed by the actual DOS filename.

If the file resides in a different storage area than the default disk and directory, a *disk* clause may be used to change the drive letter and directory path. To open a disk file for appending, use the built-in predicate *openappend*. Two other Turbo Prolog predicates, *openread* and *openwrite,* may be used for segregated disk read and disk write operations.

References:

openread; openwrite; openappend; closefile

openread

Use:

The openread predicate opens a disk file for reading, with a specified symbolic name (synonym).

Format:

openread(synonym,filename)

Examples:

openread("records.med")
openread"accounts.dat")

Comments:

The Turbo Prolog predicate *openread* is used in a disk input/output operation to open a file for reading. The argument consists of the symbolic filename (synonym) by which the file will be referenced, followed by the actual DOS filename.

If the file resides in a different storage area than the default disk and directory, a disk clause may be used to change the drive letter and directory path. To open a disk file for appending, use the built-in predicate *openappend*.

Figure 3.17 illustrates the use of openread in a disk read operation.

```
predicates
    test_data
    get_data
    displ_data

clauses
    test_data:-
        get_data,
        displ_data.
    get_data:-
        openread(datafile,"test.dat"),
        readdevice(datafile),
        get_data.
    displ_data:-
        not(eof(datafile)),
        readint(Result),
        writedevice(screen),
        write(Result),
        get_data.
```

Figure 3.17 Sample use of openread in Turbo Prolog

References:

readdevice; openappend; openmodify; openread; openwrite

pencolor

Use:

In Turbo Prolog, *pencolor* sets the color of the graphics pen or brush of the graphics turtle.

Examples:

```
pencolor(1)
pencolor(A)
```

Comments:

The argument consists of a foreground color value or a variable referring to a color value. The IBM PC Color Graphics Adaptor supports eight Turbo Prolog color values. Figure 3.18 lists the possible values.

Foreground Color	Value
Black	0
Blue	1
Green	2
Cyan	3
Red	4
Magenta	5
White	7
Yellow	14

Figure 3.18 Sample IBM PC color values in Turbo Prolog

Before the pen may begin to paint on the screen, a *pendown* clause must be used. The predicate *penup* terminates the turtle's drawing action. The screen must be in graphics mode.

References:

pendown; penup

pendown

Use:

In Turbo Prolog, *pendown* initiates the graphics turtle's drawing action.

Comments:

This predicate has no argument. It has the effect of painting the screen according to the color value specified in a previous *pencolor* clause. The turtle's movement on the screen is activated with the predicates forward and back; the direction is manipulated with *left* and *right* clauses, indicating the angle of rotation. The drawing action is terminated with the predicate *penup*.

References:

pencolor; penup; forward; back; left; right

penpos

Use:

In Turbo Prolog 1.1, *penpos* defines the position and direction of the graphics pen or turtle.

Format:

```
penpos(row,col,direction)
```

Examples:

```
penpos (1000,1000,30)
penpos(R,C,D)
```

Comments:

The argument consists of three integers: the first corresponding to the row number; the second to the column number of the turtle's current position on the screen; and the third integer indicating the current direction.

The clause in the first example sets the turtle at row 1000, column 1000, in a direction of 30. In the second example, the unbound variables *R, C,* and *D* will be instantiated by the values for the turtle's current position and direction.

Note that in a graphics mode, Turbo Prolog considers the screen to be divided into 32,000 rows by 32,000 columns, regardless of the screen resolution selected.

References:

left; right; forward; back

penup

Use:

In Turbo Prolog, *penup* terminates the drawing action of the graphics turtle.

Comments:

Like *pendown,* this predicate is used without an argument. It has the effect of lifting the turtle's paintbrush from the screen. The drawing action is initiated with the predicate *pendown,* and movement is controlled by clauses constructed with *forward, back, left,* and *right.*

References:

pendown

portbyte

Use:

The predicate *portbyte* sends a specified byte to a designated I/O port.

Format:

```
portbyte(port,byte)
      where port  = port number
            byte  = decimal equivalent
```

Examples:

portbyte(P,D)

Comments:

This predicate can be used both to send a byte value to a designated port and to retrieve the decimal equivalent of a byte from a port.

References:

membyte; memword

ptr_dword

Use:

The predicate *ptr_dword* determines the address and offset of a character string in memory.

Format:

```
ptr_dword(string,seg,offset)
     where string   = character string
            seg      = memory segment
            offset   = offset value
```

Examples:

ptr_dword(STRING,DS,DX)

Comments:

The argument consists of a variable referring to the designated string, a variable for the memory segment, and a variable for the offset value. When either the string variable or the segment and offset variables are bound, Turbo Prolog returns the values for the unbound variable(s).

References:

membyte; memword

random

Use:

The predicate *random* returns a random integer value.

Examples:

```
random(X)
```

Comments:

The Turbo Prolog predicate *random* is a random number generator that returns an integer between 0 and 1.

readchar

Use:

In Turbo Prolog, *readchar* reads a character from the keyboard or the current input stream.

Examples:

```
readchar(Key)
```

Comments:

The argument consists of a variable corresponding to the input character. A *readdevice* clause may be used to set or change the default input source. The normal Turbo Prolog default is the keyboard.

Hazards:

Only a single character is permissible in the argument. The character must be an ASCII text character. To read a keyboard entry in which more than one character is possible, use the predicate *readln* or *readterm*.

References:

readdevice; readln; readint; readreal; readterm

readdevice

Use:

In Turbo Prolog, *readdevice* specifies the input source for a file *read* operation, referring to the source's symbolic name (synonym).

Examples:

```
readdevice(datafile)
readdevice(input)
readdevice(keyboard)
```

Comments:

The argument of *readdevice* must consist of the input source's symbolic name, not the actual DOS filename. The symbolic name (synonym) refers to the name assigned to the file when it was opened for reading, for example, with the predicate *openread* or *openmodify*. The Turbo Prolog default input source is the keyboard.

References:

openread; openmodify; readln; readchar; readint; readreal; readterm

readint

Use:

In Turbo Prolog, *readint* reads an integer from the current input stream.

Examples:

```
readint(Entry)
readint(A)
readint(Locator)
```

Comments:

The argument must consist of an integer or a variable bound to an integer. A *readdevice* may be used to change the default input source. The Turbo Prolog default is the keyboard.

Hazards:

Only an integer is permissible in the argument. If a real number is a possible value, Prolog will round the real number to return an integer. To read a real number without rounding, use *readreal.*

References:

readdevice; readreal; readchar; readln

readln

Use:

In Turbo Prolog, *readln* reads a line of text or data from the current input stream.

Examples:

```
readln(Entry)
readln(X)
readln(Pname)
```

Comments:

The argument must consist of a character string or a variable corresponding to a character string. Turbo Prolog defines a line as string terminated with a carriage return (ASCII decimal 13 or 0D in hex). A *readdevice* clause may be used to set or alter the current input stream. The Turbo Prolog default is the keyboard.

References:

readdevice; readchar; readint; readreal; readterm

readreal

Use:

In Turbo Prolog, *readreal* reads a real number from the current input stream.

Examples:

```
readreal(Entry)
readreal(Result)
readreal(X)
```

Comments:

The argument must consist of a real number or a variable bound to a real number. A *readdevice* clause may be used to set or alter the current input stream. The Turbo Prolog default is the keyboard.

Hazards:

Only a real number is permissible in the argument. This predicate may not be used to read a string containing alpha characters.

References:

readdevice; readint; readchar; readln; readterm

readterm

Use:

The *readterm* predicate reads a Turbo Prolog term previously created with a *write* clause.

Format:

```
readterm(dom,term)
      where dom    = domain
            term   = clause to be read
```

Examples:

readterm(dbasedom,Clause)

Comments:

The argument consists of the domain to which the source term belongs and a variable specifying the term. A *readdevice* clause may be used to establish the source.

References:

write; readln

removewindow

Use:

In Turbo Prolog, *removewindow* deletes the most recently referenced window.

Comments:

This predicate does not require an argument.

References:

makewindow

renamefile

Use:

The *renamefile* predicate changes the name of a disk file in the default storage area.

Format:

renamefile(oldname,newname)

Examples:

renamefile("newbatch.rec","batch.rec")
renamefile(Trend,"trend.dat")
renamefile(X,Filename)

Comments:

The argument consists of the existing DOS filename (oldname) or a variable bound to an existing filename, and the new filename (newname) or its corresponding variable. The old name must appear first, as in the DOS *ren* command. (Note that the order is precisely the opposite in CP/M's *ren* command.)

The first example renames *newbatch.rec* to *batch.rec,* presumably after an append operation. The clause in the second example renames the file bound to the variable *Trend* to the DOS filename *trend.dat.* In the last example, the file bound to *X* will be changed to the filename bound to *Y.*

Hazards:

The file must reside in the default storage area. A prior *disk* clause may be required to set or alter the default drive letter and directory path.

References:

disk; dir

---

retract

Use:

The predicate *retract* removes a clause from the top of the current database.

Examples:

```
retract(suspected(_))
retract(Clause)
```

Comments:

The Prolog predicate *retract* removes a previously asserted fact from the RAM database. Each time the clause succeeds by matching a variable in the argument, the corresponding fact at the top of the database is removed. This predicate is necessary to prevent redundant goal pursuit after new clauses have been added with *asserta* or *assertz.*

The argument consists of the factual expression to be removed. In the first example, the first fact constructed with the predicate *suspected* will be removed from the database, assuming that at least one such fact was previously asserted. In the second example, the variable *Clause* must be instantiated with a clause.

The following routine illustrates the use of *retract* to clear the database for the processing of new data.

```
new_data:-
        retract(trend(_,_)),
        fail.
```

When Prolog pursues the goal new_data, the first previously asserted clause for *trend* containing any two objects in the argument will be deleted. The *fail* causes Prolog to backtrack until all the qualifying clauses have been deleted.

References:

asserta; assertz; fail

right

Use:

In Turbo Prolog, *right* rotates the current direction of the graphics turtle or pen, a specified number of degrees to the right.

Examples:

```
right(45)
right(X)
```

Comments:

This predicate is used to change the direction of the drawing pen on the screen in a graphics mode. The argument consists of an integer representing the desired angle in degrees, or a variable corresponding to the angle.

References:

left; back; forward

save

Use:

The predicate *save* stores the contents of the current RAM database in a disk file.

Examples:

```
save("current.dat")
save(C)
```

Comments:

The Turbo Prolog predicate *save* outputs the contents of the current database to a specified disk file. The argument consists of the output DOS filename, enclosed in double quotation marks, or a variable bound to the filename.

Use *save* to capture new clauses added to the database with *asserta* or *assertz*.

References:

consult; asserta; assertz

scr_attr

Use:

In Turbo Prolog, *scr_attr* defines the video attribute for a single character position.

Format:

```
scr_attr(row,col,value)
```

Examples:

```
scr_attr(12,0,112)
scr_attr(X,Y,33)
scr_attr(R,C,V)
```

Comments:

Use *scr_attr* to assign or alter the video attribute of a single character position. The argument consists of three integers, the initial pair representing the row and column. The third integer or variable corresponds to the attribute value. If the row and column are known, the third variable in the argument will be bound to the current attribute value. If all three variables are known, or if specific values are supplied in the argument, the specified attribute value will be assigned to the character position.

The clause in the first example sets the character position at row 12, column 0 to inverse video (attribute value 112). In the second example, the row and column bound to *X* and *Y* will be set to attribute 33. If the row and column are known, Turbo Prolog will bind a variable in the third argument position to the current attribute value.

Figure 3.4 lists several examples of Turbo Prolog video attribute values. To assign or alter the video attribute of the entire screen, use the built-in predicate *attribute*. Use *window_attr* to reference the attribute of a window, or use *field_attr* for a specified string length.

References:

attribute; window_attr; field_attr

scr_char

Use:

In Turbo Prolog, *scr_char* reads or writes a displayed character.

Format:

```
scr_char(row,col,character)
```

Examples:

```
scr_char(12,40,'A')
scr_char(12,40,X)
scr_char(R,C,X)
```

Comments:

Use this predicate to display a single character at a specified row and column, or to read a currently displayed character. The argument consists of three objects: the first two must be integers referencing the row and column numbers; the third represents the character.

In the first example, the character A will be displayed at row 12, column 40. In the second example, the variable *X* will be bound to whatever character is currently displayed at row 12, column 40.

References:

scr_attr

scroll

Use:

In Turbo Prolog 1.1, this predicate scrolls the display vertically or horizontally inside the current window.

Format:

```
scroll(rows,cols)
        where rows  = number of rows
              cols  = number of columns
```

Examples:

```
scroll(10,_)
scroll(_,20)
```

Comments:

The argument consists of two objects: the first representing the number of rows and the second corresponding to the number of columns. Either number may be positive or negative. A positive number of rows scrolls forward (page down), whereas a negative number scrolls backward (page up). A positive number of columns scrolls horizontally left (page right), and a negative number scrolls right (page left).

References:

window_str; field_str; display

shiftwindow

Use:

In Turbo Prolog, *shiftwindow* transfers the dialog to a specified window.

Examples:

```
shiftwindow(3)
shiftwindow(N)
```

Comments:

This predicate supports Turbo Prolog's elegant windowing facilities. The argument consists of the window number assigned to a window previously created with makewindow. Only an integer may be used to assign or reference a window number. The *shiftwindow* predicate transfers all succeeding screen write operations to the designated window.

References:

makewindow

sound

Use:

In Turbo Prolog, *sound* produces an audio tone of specified length and frequency.

Format:

```
sound(length,frequency)
```

Examples:

```
sound(50,523)
sound(X,Y)
```

Comments:

The argument consists of two integers: the first represents the length of the tone in hundredths of a second; the remaining integer denotes the frequency in cycles per second, or Hertz. Figure 3.19 lists the frequencies of some common notes. In the first example, a middle C (262 Hz) will be produced for one-half second (50 hundredths). In the second example, the frequency bound to *Y* will be produced for the duration bound to *X*.

Hazards:

Note that though this clause resembles normal BASIC sound syntax, it is substantially different. In BASIC, the *sound* statement:

```
SOUND 500,6.88
```

creates a 500-Hz tone at a length of 6.88 ticks per second. Not only is the length-frequency ordering reversed, but the measure of tone length is altogether incompatible. Only an integer may be used to specify the tone length in a Turbo Prolog sound clause. Hence, a length of 6.88 ticks per second is equivalent to 1/6.88, or approximately 15 hundredths. The comparable Turbo Prolog clause for the BASIC instruction above would therefore be:

```
sound(15,500)
```

To determine the correct tone length for a given tempo, simply divide the desired tempo (beats per minute) by 60, then divide the result into 100. Thus, to achieve a tempo of 240, the tone length would be equal to 100/(240/60), or 25 hundredths of a second. Some sample tone lengths are shown in Figure 3.20.

Low						High	
C	131	C	262	C	523	C	1047
D	147	D	294	D	587	D	1175
E	165	E	230	E	659	E	1319
F	175	F	349	F	698	F	1397
G	196	G	392	G	784	G	1568
A	220	A	440	A	880	A	1760
B	247	B	494	B	988	B	1976

Figure 3.19 Frequencies of common notes

Tempo	Tone Length
Larghissimo	150
Largo	100
Adagio	79
Andante	56
Moderato	50
Allegro	36
Presto	29

Figure 3.20 Sample tone lengths for various tempos

storage

Use:

In Turbo Prolog, *storage* determines the available stack, heap, and trail for run-time.

Format:

storage(Stack,Heap,Trail)

Examples:

storage(S,H,T)

Comments:

The argument consists of three real numbers or variables whose bound values are real numbers: the first corresponds to the available stack size, the second the available heap size, and the third the available trail size.

str_char

Use:

The *str_char* predicate converts a string to a character or a character to a string.

Format:

str_char(String,Character)

Examples:

str_char(S,C)

Comments:

The Turbo Prolog predicate *str_char* may be used to convert a string whose contents are a single character to a character atom. Similarly, it may also be used to convert a character to a single-character string. The argument consists of two objects: the first representing the string; the second representing the character.

In the example, if *S* is known, the character in the string bound to *S* would be output as the character atom *C*. If, on the other hand, *C* were known, the character bound to *C* would be output as string *S*. If both *S* and *C* are known, the goal fails unless they contain the same character.

Hazards:

The string bound to the first object in the argument must contain only a single character. The length of a string can be determined in Turbo Prolog with the built-in predicate str_len.

References:

str_int; str_real; str_len

str_int

Use:

In Turbo Prolog, *str_int* converts a specified string from decimal to binary, or binary to decimal. The binary equivalent must be an integer.

Format:

str_int(String,Integer)

Examples:

str_int(S,I)

Comments:

The argument consists of two objects, the first representing the string and the second an integer. This predicate binds the first object to the decimal equivalent of the specified string and binds the second object to the corresponding binary equivalent.

In the example, if S is known, the variable I will be bound to the binary equivalent of the string bound to S. Conversely, if I is known, S will be bound to the decimal equivalent of the binary value bound to I. If both S and I are known, the goal fails unless the decimal string bound to S is equivalent to the binary representation bound to I.

References:

str_real; str_char

str_len

Use:

In Turbo Prolog, *str_len* determines the length of a string.

Format:

str_len(String,Length)

Examples:

str_len(S,L)

Comments:

This predicate may be used to determine or test for the length of a specified string. The argument consists of two objects, the first representing the string and the second corresponding to the length. In the example, if S is known, L will be bound to the length of the string represented by S. If both S and L are known, the goal fails unless the exact length of string S is the integer bound to L.

References:

str_char

str_real

Use:

In Turbo Prolog, *str_real* converts a specified string from decimal to binary, or from binary to decimal. The binary equivalent must be a real number.

Format:

str_real(String,Real)

Examples:

str_int(S,R)

Comments:

The argument consists of two objects, the first representing the string and the second a real number. This predicate binds the first object to the decimal equivalent of the specified string and binds the second object to the corresponding binary equivalent.

In the example, if *S* is known, the variable *I* will be bound to the binary equivalent of the string bound to *S*. Conversely, if *I* is known, *S* will be bound to the decimal equivalent of the binary value bound to *I*. If both *S* and *I* are known, the goal fails unless the decimal string bound to *S* is equivalent to the binary representation bound to *I*.

References:

str_int

system

Use:

In Turbo Prolog, *system* executes a DOS command from within a program.

Examples:

```
system(" \ system \ chkdsk a:")
system("copy \ work \ *.dat \ storage")
system(Command_str)
system(" ")
```

Comments:

The built-in predicate *system* permits operating system commands to be executed from within a Turbo Prolog command. The argument consists of the DOS command string, enclosed in double quotation marks, or a variable bound to the command string.

The clause in the first example uses the CHKDSK command to check the available storage on the disk in drive A. Note that the directory path must be given if the command requires access to a transient file in a storage area other than the default drive and directory. If a resident command is specified, as in the second example, the directory path may be omitted. In the third example, the DOS command bound to the variable Command_str will be executed. The fourth example illustrates a clause for accessing the operating system command line without specifying a command name. To exit from DOS and return to the current program, enter EXIT at the DOS command line.

References:

exit

text

Use:

In Turbo Prolog, *text* changes the display mode of the entire screen to text mode.

Comments:

This predicate does not require an argument. The goal succeeds even if the default text mode has not previously been altered.

References:

graphics

time

Use:

In Turbo Prolog, *time* sets or determines the current time, according to the system clock.

Format:

```
time(hr,min,sec,hundr)
     where hr      = hour in military time
           min     = minute
           sec     = second
           hundr   = hundredth of a second
```

Examples:

```
time(14,10,00,00)
time(H,M,_,_)
```

Comments:

Use *time* to set the system clock within a program or to retrieve the current time from the system clock. The argument consists of four objects, all of which represent integers. The first corresponds to the hour in military time, that is, from 1 to 23. The second object designates the minute, the third the second, and the fourth the hundredth of a second.

The clause in the first example sets the system clock to 2:10 P.M. The second example will output the current hour and minute, ignoring the second and hundreth of a second.

To set or retrieve the date in Turbo Prolog, use the built-in predicate *date*.

References:

date

trace

Use:

In Turbo Prolog, *trace* toggles the compiler trace routine.

Examples:

```
trace(on)
trace(off)
```

Comments:

Use *trace* to monitor execution from within a program. The argument consists of one object, either on or off. Tracing is activated according to the Turbo Prolog compiler's default trace mode. The trace compiler directive must be set at the top of the compiler in order to toggle the trace function with this predicate.

upper_lower

Use:

In Turbo Prolog, *upper_lower* converts a string of upper-case characters to lower-case, or a string of lower-case characters to upper-case.

Format:

```
upper_lower(string1,string2)
        where string1  = upper-case string
              string2  = lower-case string
```

Examples:

```
upper_lower(Str1,Str2)
```

Comments:

The predicate *upper_lower* may be used to convert a string consisting of upper-case characters to a comparable lower-case string. Conversely, it may also be used to convert lower-case to upper-case. The argument consists of two objects, the first representing the upper-case string and the second corresponding to the lower-case string.

In the first example, if S1 is known, the characters in the bound string will be output as a lower-case string bound to S2. If S2 is known, the lower-case string will be output as an upper-case string bound to S1. If both S1 and S2 are known, the goal fails unless S1 is the upper-case equivalent of S2.

References:

str_int; str_real

window_attr

Use:

In Turbo Prolog, *window_attr* assigns a video attribute to the current window.

Examples:

```
window_attr(7)
window_attr(A)
```

Comments:

This predicate is unique to Turbo Prolog and supports the compiler's elegant windowing and graphics facilities. The argument must consist of an integer corresponding to the desired video attribute value or a variable bound to that value.

The clause in the first example sets the attribute of the most recently referenced window to inverse video (attribute value 7). In the second example, the variable *A* must be bound to a specific attribute value. Figure 3.4 lists several examples of video attributes. The method of computing the screen attribute value is discussed in Section 5.

Hazards:

This predicate does not provide for a window number in the argument. Hence, it takes effect only on the window in which the current dialog (i.e., cursor position and screen write operations) is taking place. To transfer the dialog from one window to another, use the built-in predicate *shiftwindow*.

References:

shiftwindow; makewindow; attr; scr_attr

window_str

Use:

In Turbo Prolog, *window_str* displays or retrieves a character string in the current window.

Examples:

```
window_str(String1)
```

Comments:

Use *window_str* to display a specified string in the current window or to retrieve a string currently displayed. The argument consists of one object corresponding to the desired string. In the example, if *String1* is not yet bound, the string currently displayed in the active window will be bound to it. If String1 is known, its contents will be displayed in the active window.

Hazards:

The displayed string will be truncated according to the dimensions of the window. For cosmetic purposes, the string should contain a carriage-return character on each line at a point prior to the right edge of the window. Take care to assure that the total number of characters in the string, including blank-space characters, does not exceed the total number of character positions in the window.

Note that the argument does not provide for a window number. Before attempting to bind a displayed string, it may be necessary to insert a prior shiftwindow clause to transfer the point of reference to the desired window.

References:

field_str; shiftwindow

write

Use:

This predicate writes a string, a value, or a series of strings and values to the current output stream, usually the display screen.

Examples:

write("Please enter your selection: ")
write(" \ 13')
write(Conclusion)
write("My conclusion is ",C)

Comments:

The Prolog predicate *write* is used to print characters or values on the display screen or to write data to a specified file or other destination. The argument consists of the string or value, or a variable corresponding to the string or value. An object of the string domain must be enclosed in double quotation marks. An ASCII decimal value for a single character must be preceded by a backslash character and appear enclosed in double quotation marks. The default output device is the screen. The destination may be altered with a prior *writedevice* clause.

To write a series of objects to the output stream, separate each object with a comma. Double quotation marks must appear at the start and end of each literal string in the series. Figure 3.21 shows a sample menu routine using *write*.

```
predicates
      menu
      selection

goal
      menu,
      selection,
      keypressed.

clauses
   menu:-
      makewindow(1,7,7,"Main Menu",2,15,20,50),
      nl,nl,nl,nl,nl,
      write("  Please select from the options below.",'\n','\n'),
      write("     1. Add a fact to the knowledge base.",'\n'),
      write("     2. Display the facts in the knowledge base.",'\n'),
      write("     3. Conduct a consultation.",'\n'),
      write("     4. Quit.",'\n'),
      nl,nl,
      sound(5,200).
   selection:-
      cursor(14,20),
      readln(Entry),
      write(Entry).
```

Figure 3.21 Sample use of write in a menu routine

Hazards:

Any characters inadvertently imposed between the quotation marks will be interpreted as part of the output string. Consider the following clause:

```
write("Diagnosis : ,X,nl")
```

The obvious intent is to print "Diagnosis : " followed by the object bound to *X* and a carriage return. Unfortunately, as written, the clause would actually output the following:

```
Diagnosis : ,X,nl
```

The correct format for the *write* clause is as follows:

```
write("Diagnosis : ",X,nl)
```

References:

writedevice; writef

Write device missing!

writef

Use:

In Turbo Prolog, *writef* writes a formatted string to the current output stream.

Format:

```
writef(string,object,object...object)
```

Examples:

```
writef("Blood test: −%20  Count: %8.1f \ n",T,C)
```

Comments:

The predicate *writef* permits output to be formatted according to embedded format codes. The argument consists of the formatted string followed by the objects to which the string applies. The clause in the example outputs the string "Blood test: Count:" using the objects *T* and *C*. The format codes specify that the values bound to *T* will be no longer than 20 characters, left-justified (− %20); and that the values bound to *C* will be 8 characters, right-justified, consisting of fixed decimals with one decimal point displayed (%8.1f). The string format codes are defined as follows:

% Embedded format code
− Justify left
f Fixed decimal notation
e Exponential notation
g Shortest possible format

The % code preceded by an optional hyphen indicates that the value will be left-justified. If no hyphen precedes the % code, the default is right-justified. The number following the % code represents the maximum field length. If a decimal is to be displayed, the number of decimal points is added after the field length. The code for fixed decimal (f), exponential (e), or shortest format (g) is the last character of the embedded format code.

The following example illustrates the embedded format codes used in a *writef* clause.

```
writef(" −%12   −%18   %7.2f \ n"),Territory, Manager, Sales")
```

The values for Territory will be left-justified (− %) in a 12-character field (12). The values for Territory will be left-justified in an 18-character field (− %18). The values for Sales will be right-justified (%) in a 7-character field with two decimals (%7.2). All the values for Sales will be expressed as fixed decimals.

Hazards:

For cosmetic purposes, it may be desirable to include blank character spaces in the string to separate each column in the array. Remember to include a carriage-return character (\ n or \ 13) at the end of each line.

References:

write

Input/Output

- **File Access**
- **File Management**
- **Asserting Facts**

File Access

Files may be accessed in a Prolog program by one of two methods. One involves consulting a file from storage. The other involves opening files for conventional read/write operations.

Consulting a File

Figure 4.1 illustrates an algorithm for consulting a file in storage. Prolog consults a file by reading the entire contents into the database. The clauses in the consulted file are treated as if they were normal factual expressions contained in the program listing.

```
consult file.
process clauses:-
      predicate(object,object...object),
      .
      .
      predicate(object,object...object).
```

Figure 4.1 Algorithm for consulting a file

The built-in predicate *consult* is standard in most versions of Prolog and is used to read the contents of a file into the current database. The argument consists of the name of the file to be consulted or a variable bound to the filename. As an example, the clause:

```
consult("rules.txt")
```

reads the DOS file *file.text* from the default drive and directory path and adds the contents. Note that a filename is technically a string and must be enclosed in double quotation marks. For the clause to succeed, the file must contain valid Prolog factual expressions. If a syntax error is encountered at run-time, the clause fails.

The following clause illustrates the use of a variable in the argument:

```
consult(F)
```

In this example, the variable *F* must be bound to a valid DOS filename or the clause will fail.

Figure 4.2 demonstrates a file consultation in Turbo Prolog.

```
domains
  varietal,vineyard,dryness            = string
  vintage                              = integer
database
  stock(varietal,vineyard,dryness,vintage)
predicates
  get_vintage
goal
  consult("cellar.dat"),
  get_vintage.
clauses
  get_vintage:-
        write("Varietal: "),
        readln(X),
        stock(X,_,_,Y),
        write(X,"The available vintage is ",Y),
        keypressed.
```

Figure 4.2 File consultation in Turbo Prolog

Read/Write Operations

In addition to consulting a file, Prolog provides for conventional file I/O involving reading or writing data in a program. Figure 4.3 illustrates an algorithm for file I/O in Prolog.

```
write to file:-
      open file for writing,
      address output destination,
      write data,
      close file.

read from file:-
      open file for reading,
      address input source,
      read data,
      close file.
```

Figure 4.3 Algorithm for conventional file I/O

The default output destination in most Prolog systems is the console screen. Before a file may be written to, the output stream must be altered to address the desired file as the destination. All subsequent write operations will be directed by the output stream to the addressed file, until the stream is re-altered. Some versions of Prolog (e.g., Turbo Prolog) also require the output file to be opened in a mode for writing.

When the write operation is terminated, the file is closed so that it may be opened again in the future.

An identical procedure with an inverse data stream is used to read data from a file. The default input source is normally the keyboard. The stream is altered by addressing the desired input source, namely, the source file. If required by the language version, the file is opened in a mode for reading. After the data has been read into the current input stream, the file is closed so that it may be reopened in the future.

File I/O in Standard Prolog

Standard versions of Prolog have four basic predicates for file I/O (for Turbo Prolog I/O, see the next topic). Their syntax and use are summarized in Figure 4.4.

	Example	Use
see	ask(filename)	Change input device to the named file, and open for reading.
tell	tell(filename)	Change output device to the named file, and open for writing.
read	read(Text)	Input Text from the file.
write	write(Text)	Output Text to the file.
seen	seen(filename)	Close file after reading.
told	told(filename)	Close file after writing.

Figure 4.4 Standard Prolog I/O predicates

The built-in predicate *see* assigns a file as the default input source and opens the file for reading with read. The predicate *seen* is used to close the file after reading. In contrast, the predicate *tell* assigns a file as the default output destination and opens the file for writing with *write*. A clause constructed with the predicate *told* is used to close the file after writing.

Figure 4.5 illustrates Standard Prolog routines for file read and write operations.

```
read_text:-
        write('Name of file: '),
        read(Name),
        see(Name),
        read(Text),
        write(Text),
        seen.

write_text:-
        write('Name of file: '),
        read(Name),
        tell(Name),
        read(Text),
        write(Text),
        told.
```

Figure 4.5 Standard routines for file read and write operations

Assume, as an example, that Datafile is a variable bound to a file to which information is to be written. The following sequence opens the file for writing, writes data into the file, and closes the file so it may be reopened in the future.

```
tell(Datafile),
write(Data),
told(Datafile).
```

In this illustration, Data is a variable bound to the string or to the value(s) to be written to the file.

File I/O in Turbo Prolog

Not coincidentally, file I/O conventions in Turbo Prolog resemble those in Turbo Pascal. In concept, they are similar to read and write procedures in standard versions of Prolog, except that the Turbo Prolog predicates designed for this purpose are more specific. Separate predicates are used to alter the current data stream and to open a file for reading or writing. In addition, Turbo Prolog recognizes several different open-file modes, depending on whether the file will be read from, written to, appended, or modified.

Figure 4.6 lists the Turbo Prolog file I/O predicates with their respective uses.

```
openread(synonym,"readfrom.fil")

   /* Opens the DOS file readfrom.fil for reading,
      assigning the symbolic name synonym. */

readdevice(synonym)

   /* Assigns the file synonym as the current input
      source. */

openwrite(synonym,"writeto.fil")

   /* Opens the DOS file writeto.fil for writing,
      assigning the symbolic name synonym. */

writedevice(synonym)

   /* Assigns the file synonym as the current output
      destination. */

openappend(synonym,"appendto.fil")

   /* Opens the DOS file appendto.fil for appending,
      assigning the symbolic name synonym. */

openmodify(synonym,"modify.fil")

   /* Opens the DOS file modify.fil for reading and
      writing, assigning the symbolic name synonym. */

closefile(synonym)

   /* Closes the file synonym after reading or writing. */
```

Figure 4.6 Turbo Prolog file I/O predicates

The antonyms *readdevice* and *writedevice* are used to alter the current data stream. Turbo Prolog refers to a current input source as the read device; hence the built-in predicate *readdevice* alters the input stream by assigning a file as the current input source. Similarly, Turbo Prolog considers a current output destination to be the write device; thus, *writedevice* alters the output stream by assigning a file as the current output destination.

The argument of either predicate must consist of the file's symbolic name, or synonym. The synonym is defined in a file domain declaration and assigned when the file is opened for reading or writing. In addition to user-defined synonyms, Turbo Prolog also recognizes the built-in synonyms screen and printer as write devices and keyboard as a read device.

The four Turbo Prolog open-file modes are *read, write, append*, and *modify*. A separate predicate must be used to open a file for each type of operation. As a predicate, *closefile* closes a file, regardless of whether the file was opened for reading, writing, or appending. Its clause always succeeds, even if the named file was not previously opened.

Figure 4.7 illustrates conventional file I/O in a Turbo Prolog program.

```
domains
     descr           = string
     part_num        = integer
     cost            = real
     file            = partlist
     part            = record(part_num,descr,cost)

predicates
     part_cost
     find_part(file)

goal
     part_cost.

clauses
     part_cost:-
          makewindow(1,7,7,"Part Cost",0,0,15,30),
          write("Part: "),
          readln(Descr),
          openread(partlist,"parts.dat"),
          readdevice(partlist),
          find_part(partlist),
          readterm(part,record(Part_Num,Descr,Cost),nl,nl,
          write("Part No.     : ",Part_Num),nl,
          write("Description  : ",Descr),nl,
          write("Cost         : ",Cost),nl,
          keypressed.
     find_part(_).
     find_part(P):-
          not(eof(P)),
          find_part(P).
```

Figure 4.7 Conventional file I/O in a Turbo Prolog program

File Editing in Turbo Prolog

A particularly elegant characteristic of Turbo Prolog is the provision of a full-function, built-in screen editor that may be accessed from within a compiled program during execution. The editor supports a broad range of word processor-like commands, most of which are based on WordStar conventions. However, unlike WordStar, the editor outputs unformatted ASCII text, and thus it can be used to create or edit virtually any type of file which may be accessed by a Turbo Prolog program.

Within a program, the editor may be invoked with the built-in predicate *edit*. The argument consists of the text string to be edited (input string), followed by a reference to the output string. Consider, for instance, the following clause:

```
edit(Input,Output)
```

This clause invokes the screen editor and loads the string bound to the variable Input. When the editor is terminated with an F10 key press, the edited string will be bound to the variable Output. In the following variation, the input string is defined with no characters:

```
edit(" ",Output)
```

The effect is to activate the screen editor for creation of a new string which will be bound to Output. Any string output by the screen editor may be written to a file, using the Turbo Prolog conventions for file I/O. Figure 4.8 illustrates a technique for writing to a disk file using the built-in screen editor.

```
domains
  file  = document

predicates
  edit_file
  read_file
  display_text

clauses
  edit_file:-
        makewindow(1,7,7,"Screen Editor",0,0,25,80),
        write("Name of file: "),readln(Name),
        edit("",Text),
        openwrite(document,Name),
        writedevice(document),
        write(Text),
        closefile(document).

  read_file:-
        makewindow(1,7,7,"View Mode",0,0,25,80),
        write("Name of File to View: "),readln(Name),
        openread(document,Name),
        readdevice(document),
        display_text,
        closefile(document).

  display_text:-
                file_str(Name,I),
                display(I).
```

Figure 4.8 Using the built-in editor to write to a disk file

The Turbo Prolog editor recognizes WordStar conventions for cursor positioning, text editing, block maneuvers, and search-and-replace operations. Figure 4.9 summarizes the editor commands. On an IBM PC, the F function keys are supported, as well.

Function	Command
Toggle insert mode	Ctrl-V
Delete character right	Ctrl-G
Delete character left	Del
Delete word right	Ctrl-T
Delete current line	Ctrl-Y
Mark beginning of block	Ctrl-KB
Mark end of block	Ctrl-KK
Copy block	Ctrl-KC
Move block	Ctrl-KV
Delete block	Ctrl-KY
Search and replace	Ctrl-QA
Find string	Ctrl-QF
Quit	F10

Figure 4.9 Sample Turbo Prolog editing commands

File Management

Turbo Prolog provides two methods of file management within a program. One involves the use of built-in predicates for directory access and file handling, including facilities for saving, renaming, and deleting files. The other technique involves accessing DOS from within a program, enabling the invocation of any DOS command or execution file. Turbo Prolog also supports the use of BIOS interrupts for file handling.

File-Handling Predicates

Figure 4.10 lists the Turbo Prolog file-handling predicates for managing disk files.

```
dir             /* Displays or searches a directory. */

disk            /* Sets or retrieves the default drive
                   and directory path. */

existfile       /* Searches the default directory for
                   a specified file. */

save            /* Saves a file in the default storage area. */

renamefile      /* Renames a file in the default storage
                   area. */

deletefile      /* Deletes a file in the default storage
                   area. */
```

Figure 4.10 Turbo Prolog file-handling predicates

Three of the Turbo Prolog file-handling predicates are directory facilities. The *dir* predicate displays a file directory based on a specified DOS directory path, file specification, and filename. Consider, for example, the following clause:

dir(" \applications \gexpert","invest*.pro",_)

This clause is equivalent to the DOS command

C>dir \applications \expert \invest*.pro

Identical results are also achieved with this Turbo Prolog variation:

dir(" \applications \expert","invest*.pro",_)

The predicate *existfile* may be used to search a directory for a specified filename.

The sequence:

disk(" \ applications \ expert"),
existfile("invest2.pro").

changes the default directory path and searches for the DOS file *invest2.pro.* For the sequence to succeed, two conditions must be met:

1. The specified directory path must exist on the default or named drive.

2. The specified DOS filename must exist in the named subdirectory.

DOS files may also be saved, renamed, or deleted within a Turbo Prolog program. The predicate *save* stores the current data on disk in a specified DOS file. The argument consists of the DOS filename enclosed in double quotation marks. For example:

```
save("new.dat")
```

Alternatively, the argument may consist of a variable bound to the filename, as in the following:

```
save(Current)
```

The predicate *renamefile* renames a file in the default storage area. The clause:

```
renamefile("new.dat","current.dat")
```

produces identical results to the DOS command:

```
C>ren new.dat current.dat
```

A bound variable may be used in the argument to reference either the source file or the target file. For example:

```
renamefile(Current,"perform.dat")
```

Similarly, the built-in predicate *deletefile* deletes a DOS file. The clause:

```
deletefile("work.fil")
```

produces identical results to the DOS command:

```
C>del work.fil
```

Alternatively, a bound variable may be used to reference the object file. For example:

```
deletefile(Work)
```

erases the disk file whose DOS filename is bound to the variable Work.

Accessing DOS in a Turbo Prolog Program

A second method of file handling involves accessing DOS from within a Turbo Prolog program. The built-in predicate system accesses DOS and executes a valid command file or execution file named in the argument. The argument consists of the desired DOS command enclosed in double quotation marks, as in the following example:

```
system("ren new.dat current.dat")
```

The string containing the DOS command may be referenced by a variable. For example, the clause:

```
system(Command)
```

succeeds if the variable Command is bound to a string containing a valid DOS command in executable syntax.

Asserting Facts

A third type of Prolog I/O, asserting new data in a program, deserves separate consideration.

The sister predicates *asserta* and *assertz* are used to add new clauses to the current database. The letters a and z denote the top and bottom of the file, respectively. Most versions of Prolog support both of these predicates (an exception is Micro-Prolog, in which ADDCL is used to add clauses to the database).

The argument consists of a compound object equating to the construction of the clauses to be asserted. For example, the clause:

```
asserta(suspected(Organism))
```

adds clauses contructed with suspected as the predicate and a single object in the argument. The following facts would be considered valid, and thus would be inserted at the top of the current program database.

```
suspected("E. coli")
suspected("P. aeruginosa")
suspected(S. auerus")
```

Conversely, the clause:

```
assertz(valid(Object,Value))
```

would place clauses with valid as the predicate and two objects in the argument at the end of the current program database.

After one or more clauses have been asserted, they remain in the current database for the duration of execution. To resolve the goal(s) using new data, Prolog must first be told to delete the assertions from the database. The predicate retract is used for this purpose in most versions of Prolog, including Turbo Prolog. (In Micro Prolog, DELCL is used to delete asserted clauses.) The argument consists of a compound object equating to the construction of the previously asserted clause(s).

As an example, the clause:

```
retract(suspected(_))
```

deletes the first clause in the database constructed in the format suspected(Organism). The anonymous variable (_) assures that any facts with suspected as the predicate will be removed from the database.

In the clause:

```
retract(valid(Object,Value)),fail
```

the trailing *fail* enforces backtracking until all the qualifying expressions have been deleted.

Figure 4.11 illustrates the use of *asserta* and *retract* in an expert system constructed with Turbo Prolog.

```
domains
  value       = symbol
  years       = integer

database
  habits(value,value,value,value,value)

predicates
  longevity(years)
  prediction
  new_data

goal
  prediction.

clauses
  longevity(75):-
        habits(a,a,a,a,a).
```

(continued)

```
longevity(72):-
    habits(a,a,a,a,b) or
    habits(a,a,a,b,a) or
    habits(a,a,b,a,a) or
    habits(a,b,a,a,a) or
    habits(b,a,a,a,a).
longevity(67):-
    habits(a,a,a,b,b) or
    habits(a,a,b,a,b) or
    habits(a,b,a,a,b) or
    habits(b,a,a,a,b) or
    habits(a,b,b,a,a) or
    habits(b,b,a,a,a) or
    habits(a,a,b,b,a).
longevity(62):-
    habits(a,a,b,b,b) or
    habits(a,b,b,b,a) or
    habits(b,b,b,a,a) or
    habits(a,b,a,b,b) or
    habits(b,b,a,b,a) or
    habits(b,a,b,b,a) or
    habits(a,b,a,b,a).
longevity(57):-
    habits(a,b,b,b,b) or
    habits(b,a,b,b,b) or
    habits(b,b,a,b,b) or
    habits(b,b,b,a,b) or
    habits(b,b,b,b,a).
longevity(52):-
    habits(b,b,b,b,b).

prediction:-
    makewindow(1,7,7,"Longevity",0,0,25,80),
    write("Are you: "),nl,nl,
    write("  a. Female"),nl,
    write("  b. Male"),nl,nl,
    readln(Sex),
    write("Is your weight: "),nl,nl,
    write("  a. Normal for your height"),nl,
    write("  b. High or low for your height"),nl,nl,
    readln(Weight),
    write("Is your blood pressure: "),nl,
    write("  a. Normal"),nl,
    write("  b. High"),nl,nl,
    readln(BP),
    write("Do you smoke cigarettes?"),nl,nl,
    write("  a. No"),nl,
    write("  b. Yes"),nl,nl,
    readln(Smoker),
    write("Is your alcohol consumption:"),nl,nl,
    write("  a. Moderate"),nl,
    write("  b. Excessive"),nl,
    readln(Alcohol),
    asserta(habits(Sex,Weight,BP,Smoker,Alcohol)),
    longevity(X),
    nl,nl,
    write("Your predicted longevity is ",X," years."),
    nl,nl,new_data.

new_data:-
    retract(habits(_,_,_,_,_)),
    fail.
```

Figure 4.11 Using asserta and retract in an expert system

SECTION 5

Special Effects

- **Turbo Prolog Windowing Facilities**
- **Standard PC Graphics**
- **Turtle Graphics in Turbo Prolog**
- **Audio Effects with Turbo Prolog**

Turbo Prolog enhances standard Prolog programming with built-in facilities for windowing, graphics, and audio effects on the IBM PC. The windowing facilities include a set of built-in predicates for constructing and customizing windows, altering video attributes, and shifting the screen output from one window to another. The graphics facilities support standard PC graphics with several optional resolutions, as well as turtle graphics. Audio effects are support with a built-in predicate for sound generation, capable of varying both the pitch and duration of the tone.

Turbo Prolog Windowing Facilities

Figure 5.1 illustrates the Turbo Prolog predicates for window definition and handling. The predicate *makewindow* defines the basic characteristics of a program window. The argument gives each window a reference number and assigns video attributes for both the outline, or frame, and the interior. The clause also contains text for an optional header and specifications for position and size.

```
makewindow      /* Creates a window and defines its
                   specifications. */


shiftwindow     /* Transfers screen operations to a designated
                   window. */


window_attr     /* Assigns or retrieves the current video
                   attributes of the interior of a window. */


clearwindow     /* Clears the interior of a window to blank
                   spaces. */


removewindow    /* Deletes a window from the screen. */


window_str      /* Displays a specified string in a window, or
                   binds a displayed string to a variable. */
```

Figure 5.1 Turbo Prolog window-handling predicates

A clause constructed with *makewindow* has the following format:

```
makewindow(N,S,F,"Header",R,C,H,W)
   where  N          = window reference number

          S          = screen video attribute

          F          = frame video attribute

          "Header"   = text of optional header

          R          = beginning row

          C          = beginning column

          H          = height in rows

          C          = width in columns
```

Consider, as an example, the following clause:

```
makewindow(1,7,7,"Main Menu",0,0,25,80)
```

This clause succeeds by defining a window as window 1. The window number is used to reference the window in a succeeding operation, for example, the transfer of screen operations from another window. In this example, both the interior of the window and the frame are set for normal monochrome video (attribute value 7). The text "Main Menu" will appear as a header in the middle of the top crossbar of the window frame. The remaining integers define the dimensions and position of the window in relation to the overall screen. The window will begin at row 0, column 0 (the home position) and will be drawn 25 columns deep and 80 columns wide. In other words, the window will occupy the entire monitor screen on a normal IBM PC monochrome display.

Video attributes are discussed in more detail in the next topic, but in general, a window on a monochrome display may have either 7 (normal video) or 112 (inverse video) as the value for both the screen attribute and the frame attribute. Bear in mind that if the screen and frame are set to opposite attribute values, that is, one normal and the other inverse, the window frame will be invisible. With a color display, a diversity of attribute values are available for varying the color of both the interior and the frame.

An error message will be returned on compilation if the placement and dimensions of the window do not conform to the overall dimensions of the screen.

Turbo Prolog 1.1 permits a maximum of 25 windows per listing. Unless otherwise specified, all subsequent screen operations are performed inside the window, beginning at the first row and column.

The built-in predicate *shiftwindow* enables the programmer to transfer control from one window to another. The argument consists of the window reference number defined in the original makewindow clause. For instance, the clause:

```
shiftwindow(3)
```

transfers subsequent screen operations to window 3. If the window was activated previously, the cursor will appear in the same position in which it last appeared.

The built-in predicate *window_attr* changes or retrieves the current video attribute of the interior of the window. The argument consists of the desired attribute value or a variable which will be bound to the attribute value. The clause:

```
window_attr(112)
```

changes the interior of the window to inverse video (attribute value 112). Conversely, the clause:

```
window_attr(A)
```

binds the variable *A* to the current video attribute for the most recently referenced window. If, for instance, the active window is currently set for normal monochrome display, the value 7 would be bound to *A*. (For a detailed discussion of color video attributes, consult the next topic.)

When a window is active, other screen-control predicates become relative to the position and dimensions of the window. For instance, the built-in predicate *cursor* specifies a row and column position for the cursor. When the clause:

```
cursor(1,2)
```

is encountered, the cursor will be positioned at row 1, column 2 *relative to the position of the current window*. For instance, if the window in which the cursor is displayed begins at row 3, column 60, the above clause would position the cursor at actual row 4, actual column 62. Note that the outline of the window occupies the beginning row and column, so the home position of a window beginning at row 0, column 0 is actually row 1, column 1. Hence, the following sequence creates a window beginning at row 5, column 30, and positions the cursor at actual row 18, column 40 (relative row 13, relative column 10 in the window).

```
makewindow(1,7,7,"Main Menu",5,30,15,20),
display_menu,
cursor(13,10).
```

In this example, *display_menu* is a user-defined predicate that reads the contents of a text file into the active window.

The arguments of the built-in predicates *field_str* and *scr_char* also become relative to the active window. For example, in the clause:

```
field_str(2,2,12,Label)
```

a string bound to the variable Label will be placed at relative row 2, column 2 within a window. (The third integer, 12, represents the string length.) If the window begins at row 3, column 3, the actual placement of the string would be row 5, column 5, since the frame occupies the beginning row and column.

Figure 5.2 illustrates the use of built-in predicates for window handling in a Turbo Prolog program.

```
domains
  file  = document

predicates
  edit_file
  read_file
  display_text

clauses
  edit_file:-
       makewindow(1,7,7,"Screen Editor",0,0,25,80),
       write("Name of file: "),readln(Name),
       edit("",Text),
       openwrite(document,Name),
       writedevice(document),
       write(Text),
       closefile(document).
```

(continued)

```
read_file:-
     makewindow(1,7,7,"View Mode",0,0,25,80),
     write("Name of File to View: "),readln(Name),
     openread(document,Name),
     readdevice(document),
     display_text,
     closefile(document).

display_text:-
     file_str(Name,I),
     display(I).
```

Figure 5.2 Using built-in predicates for window handling

Video Attributes

The predicates *attribute*, *field_attr*, and *window_attr* are used to set or alter default video attributes. The clause:

attribute(A)

sets the value bound to *A* as the default video attribute for the entire screen. With a monochrome display, possible attributes include normal or inverse video, underlining, and high-intensity or blinking characters. Figure 5.3 lists the video attribute values for a standard monochrome display.

Display	Effect	Value
Normal	Normal	7
Normal	Underlined characters	8
Normal	High-intensity characters	15
Normal	Blinking characters	135
Inverse	Normal	112
Inverse	Underlined characters	113
Inverse	High-intensity characters	120
Inverse	Blinking characters	240

Figure 5.3 Monochrome video attributes

With a color display supported by an IBM Color/Graphics Adaptor, the attribute is computed as the sum of the background color value plus the foreground color value. The background and foreground colors are selected from the ones shown in Figure 5.4.

Background	Black	0	Gray	8	Blue	16
	Lt. blue	24	Green	32	Lt. green	40
	Cyan	48	Red	64	Lt. red	72
	Magenta	80	Lt. mg.	88	Brown	96
	Yellow	104	White	112	Int. wht.	120
Foreground	Black	0	Blue	1	Green	2
	Cyan	3	Red	4	Magenta	5
	Brown	6	White	7		

Figure 5.4 Color video attributes

For example, to specify a blue background (background value 16) and a white foreground (foreground value 7), the screen attribute value would be equal to $16 + 7 = 23$. Hence, the clause:

```
attribute(23)
```

would produce the desired color effects for all character positions on the screen. A screen attribute of 0 has the effect of clearing the screen to blanks.

Similarly, the clause:

```
field_attr(,R,C,L,71)
```

establishes a red background (64) and a white foreground (7) for the field defined at row *R*, column *C*, of field length *L*. Thus, a field at row 4, column 10, that is 64 characters in length can be highlighted with a red background using the clause:

```
field_attr(4,10,64,71)
```

Standard PC Graphics

Turbo Prolog supports a diversity of IBM PC graphics modes, depending on the type of display adaptor installed with the hardware. Built-in predicates may be used to set or alter default video attributes, define the screen resolution, establish a color for both foreground and background, and plot a point or line in a specified color at any position on the screen.

Figure 5.5 lists the Turbo Prolog predicates for standard PC graphics.

```
graphics        /* Specifies a graphics mode palette selection,

                and background color. */



dot             /* Draws a dot at a specified row and column,

                in a color determined by the default palette. */



line            /* Draws a line between two specified points,

                in a color determined by the default palette. */
```

Figure 5.5 Turbo Prolog predicates for standard graphics

The built-in predicate *graphics* initializes the screen in a graphics mode. The argument consists of three objects: graphics mode, palette selection, and background color. The graphics mode, which specifies the screen resolution, is dependent in part on the type of display adaptor installed with the hardware. For instance, graphics modes 1 and 2 apply to the IBM Color/Graphics Adaptor, whereas modes 3, 4, and 5 require an enhanced graphics adaptor, for example, a Hercules board. The palette selection may be either 0 or 1. For instance, in graphics mode 1, a value of 0 designates a green-red-yellow palette, and a value of 1 specifies a cyan-magenta-white palette. The background color may be one of 16 different values.

Consider, as an example, the following clause:

```
graphics(1,1,1)
```

This goal succeeds by initializing the screen for standard medium-resolution graphics with the IBM PC Color/Graphics Adaptor (graphics mode 1). The second integer, also 1, specifies a cyan-magenta-white palette for drawing dots or lines. The third integer selects the background color, in this case, blue (background color value 1).

Figure 5.6 lists the Turbo Prolog graphics modes along with their respective screen resolutions and supported hardware.

Adaptor	Screen	Colors	Resolution	Mode
Color/Graphics	Medium resolution	4	200 × 320	1
Color/Graphics	High resolution	Mono	200 × 640	2
Enhanced	Medium resolution	16	200 × 320	3
Enhanced	High resolution	16	200 × 640	4
Enhanced	Enhanced resolution	13	350 × 640	5

Figure 5.6 Optional Turbo Prolog graphics modes

In graphics mode 1, four colors are available, including the background color; hence, the palette consists of 3 colors. Figure 5.7 lists the values for the 16 possible background colors.

Black	0	Blue	1	Green	2	Cyan	3
Red	4	Magenta	5	Brown	6	White	7
Gray	8	Lt. blue	9	Lt. green	10	Lt. cyan	11
Lt. red	12	Lt. magenta	13	Yellow	14	Intense white	15

Figure 5.7 Background color values

After the screen has been initialized with a graphics clause, the built-in predicates dot and line may be used to draw points or lines. Placement is determined by relative values for row and column. In a graphics mode, Turbo Prolog considers the screen to be divided into 32,000 rows by 32,000 columns. A single point therefore represents 1/32,000 of the vertical or horizontal dimension of the screen. Thus, the clause:

```
dot(0,0,Color)
```

draws a dot in the extreme upper left-hand corner of the screen (provided the screen was previously initialized in a graphics mode). In this example, the variable Color must be bound to a valid color value. If Color is unbound, the clause would retrieve the default color value for the position at row 0, column 0.

Consider the following sequence:

```
graphics(1,0,14),
dot(31999,31999,2).
```

The *dot* clause would draw a dot in the extreme lower right-hand corner of the screen; the value for color (2) denotes red, since palette 0 has been selected.

Figure 5.8 illustrates the relationship between clauses constructed with *graphics* and *dot*.

```
graphics(1,1,1)        /* Medium resolution, cyan-magenta-white
                       palette, blue background */
dot(0,0,3)             /* Places a white dot at the home position */
```

```
graphics(1,0,3)        /* Medium resolution, green-red-yellow
                       palette, cyan background */
dot(16000,16000,3)     /* Places a yellow dot in the center of
                       the screen. */
```

```
graphics(1,1,2)        /* Medium resolution, cyan-magenta-white
                       palette, green background */
dot(31999,0,2)         /* Places a magenta dot at the lower left
                       hand corner of the screen. */
```

```
graphics(1,0,9)        /* Medium resolution, green-red-yellow
                       palette, light blue background */
dot(0,31999,1)         /* Places a green dot at the upper right
                       hand corner of the screen. */
```

Figure 5.8 Sample values for the predicate dot

The built-in predicate *line* draws a line between two specified points. The clause:

```
line(0,0,31999,31999,Color)
```

draws a diagonal line from the home position (row 0, column 0) to the lower right-hand corner of the screen (row 31999, column 31999). The variable Color must be bound to a valid color value. If Color is unbound, it will be bound to the color value for a line currently drawn on the screen in the specified position. As with a *dot* clause, the line color depends on the palette selection. As an example, the sequence:

```
graphics(1,1,1),
line(0,0,0,31999,3)
```

draws a horizontal white line across the top of the screen. The color value 3 corresponds to white in palette 1.

Turtle Graphics in Turbo Prolog

Standard PC graphics rely on specified static screen positions, but Turtle Graphics utilize commands referring to motion and direction. The graphics turtle is a cursor-like pen or brush that defines a trail of color as it moves along the screen. As with an actual pen on a physical drawing medium, the turtle does not draw when the pen is up—only when it is down.

Figure 5.9 illustrates an algorithm for Turtle Graphics in a Turbo Prolog program.

```
draw with turtle graphics:-
        initialize the screen,
        position the pen,
        pen down,
        start drawing,
        pen up.

start drawing:-
        specify motion,
        specify direction,
        .
        .
        .
        specify motion,
        specify direction.
```

Figure 5.9 Algorithm for Turtle Graphics

The position, motion, and direction of the turtle are defined by five of the built-in predicates listed in Figure 5.10.

```
penpos      /* Places the turtle at a specified point on the
               screen, or retrieves the current direction. */

pencolor    /* Sets the default color of the turtle's drawing
               pen. */

pendown     /* Starts the turtle drawing. */

penup       /* Stops the turtle from drawing. */

forward     /* Moves the turtle a designated number of steps
               in its current direction. */

back        /* Reverses the turtle's direction a specified
               number of steps. */

left        /* Rotates the turtle's direction a specified
               number of degrees to the left. */

right       /* Rotates the turtle's direction a specified
               number of degrees to the right. */
```

Figure 5.10 Turbo Prolog predicates for Turtle Graphics

Positioning the Turtle

A clause constructed with *penpos* defines the turtle's current placement and direction on the screen. The argument consists of three objects: the row, column, and direction. The clause:

penpos(16000,16000,Direction)

positions the turtle at the center of the screen. Note that in a graphics mode, Turbo Prolog considers the display to be divided into 32,000 rows by 32,000 columns, regardless of the actual resolution. In this example, Direction must be bound to the turtle's current direction. Conversely, if none of the variables are bound in the clause:

penpos(Current_row,Current_col,Current_dir)

the current values for the turtle's position and direction will be returned.

The color used by the turtle when it draws on the screen is specified with a *pencolor* clause. The argument consists of a color value selected from the ones listed in Figure 5.11.

Black	0	Blue	1
Green	2	Cyan	3
Red	4	Magenta	5
Brown	6	White	7

Figure 5.11 Optional pen colors for the graphics turtle

Thus, the clause:

```
pencolor(7)
```

results in a white graphic drawn on the default background color.

Drawing with the Turtle

Drawing action is initiated with *pendown,* which has no argument. Motion and direction are controlled with four built-in predicates: *forward, back, left,* and *right.*

A clause constructed with *forward* or *back* has as its argument the number of steps the turtle is to take. Each step represents a point equal in height to 1/32,000 of the screen's vertical dimension and equal in width to 1/32,000 of the horizontal dimension. The clause:

```
forward(1000)
```

will move the turtle in its current direction 100 steps, or 1/32 of the height or width of the screen. In the clause:

```
back(X)
```

the variable X must be bound to a value representing the prescribed number of steps the turtle is to take.

The current direction is specified with a clause constructed with either left or right. The argument consists of the desired angle in degrees. As an example, the clause:

left(90)

sets or alters the turtle's current direction 90 degrees to the left. Similarly,

right(X)

sets or alters the direction by the value bound to *X*. Neither left nor right will return a value for an unbound variable in the argument.

The following sequence illustrates the use of the motion and direction predicates.

```
pendown,
forward(8000),
left(45),
forward(2000)
```

In this example, the turtle moves forward 8000 steps in its current direction, then angles to the left 45 degrees and proceeds another 2000 steps.

Figure 5.12 illustrates a Turbo Prolog routine using Turtle Graphics. The turtle draws a red circle on a blue screen.

```
predicates
  ready-pen
  draw_circle

goal
  ready_pen,
  draw_circle,
  keypressed.

clauses
  ready_pen:-
          graphics(1,0,2)
          pencolor(4),
          pendown.
  draw_circle:-
          forward(1000),
          right(1),
          draw_circle.
```

Figure 5.12 Turbo Prolog routine using Turtle Graphics

Audio Effects with Turbo Prolog

IBM PC audio effects are supported in Turbo Prolog by the use of the built-in predicate sound. The argument consists of two integers, the first specifying the tone length and the second defining the frequency. Tone length is specified in hundredths of a second. As an example, the clause:

```
sound(100,1047)
```

will approximate a high C note one second in length. The frequency is given in Hertz. Figure 5.13 lists the frequencies of common musical notes.

C	131	C	262	C	523	C	1047
D	147	D	294	D	587	D	1175
E	165	E	230	E	659	E	1319
F	175	F	349	F	698	F	1397
G	196	G	392	G	784	G	1568
A	220	A	440	A	880	A	1760
B	247	B	494	B	988	B	1976

Figure 5.13 Frequencies of common notes

Musical tempo is normally given in beats per minute. Hence, the tone length value for a desired tempo may be approximated as follows:

```
Length = 100/(Beats per minute/60)
```

For example, to represent a tempo of 180 beats per minute, the tone length would be equal to 100/(180/60) or approximately 33 hundredths of a second. Figure 5.14 gives several sample tone lengths for common tempos.

Tempo	Tone Length
Larghissimo	150
Largo	100
Adagio	79
Andante	56
Moderato	50
Allegro	36
Presto	29

Figure 5.14 Sample tone lengths for various tempos

SECTION 6

Appendixes

- **ASCII Character Set**
- **Turbo Prolog Reference Summary**
- **Prolog-to-Turbo Prolog Conversion Chart**
- **Turbo Prolog Predicate Flow Patterns**
- **Turbo Prolog Graphics/Sound Values**
- **Turbo Prolog Language Summary**
- **Turbo Prolog Compiler Directives**

ASCII Character Set

char	key	dec	hex
NUL	Ctrl-@	0	00
SOH	Ctrl-A	1	01
STX	Ctrl-B	2	02
ETX	Ctrl-C	3	03
EOT	Ctrl-D	4	04
ENQ	Ctrl-E	5	05
ACK	Ctrl-F	6	06
BEL	Ctrl-G	7	07
BS	Ctrl-H	8	08
HT	Ctrl-I	9	09
LF	Ctrl-J	10	0A
VT	Ctrl-K	11	0B
FF	Ctrl-L	12	0C
CR	Ctrl-M	13	0D
SO	Ctrl-N	14	0E
SI	Ctrl-O	15	0F
DLE	Ctrl-P	16	10
DC1	Ctrl-Q	17	11
DC2	Ctrl-R	18	12
DC3	Ctrl-S	19	13
DC4	Ctrl-T	20	14
NAK	Ctrl-U	21	15
SYN	Ctrl-V	22	16
ETB	Ctrl-W	23	17
CAN	Ctrl-X	24	18
EM	Ctrl-Y	25	19
SUB	Ctrl-Z	26	1A
ESC	Esc	27	1B
FS	right cursor	28	1C
GS	left cursor	29	1D
RS	up cursor	30	1E

char	key	dec	hex
US	down cursor	31	1F
' '	Space	32	20
'!'	!	33	21
' " '	"	34	22
'#'	#	35	23
'$'	$	36	24
'%'	%	37	25
'&'	&	38	26
' ' '	'	39	27
'('	(	40	28
')''	)	41	29
'*'	*	42	2A
'+'	+	43	2B
','	,	44	2C
'='	=	45	2D
'.'	.	46	2E
' / '	/	47	2F
'0'	0	48	30
'1'	1	49	31
'2'	2	50	32
'3'	3	51	33
'4'	4	52	34
'5'	5	53	35
'6'	6	54	36
'7'	7	55	37
'8'	8	56	38
'9'	9	57	39
' : '	:	58	3A
' ; '	;	59	3B
'<'	<	60	3C
'='	=	61	3D
'>'	>	62	3E
'?'	?	63	3F
'@'	@	64	40
'A'	A	65	41
'B'	B	66	42
'C'	C	67	43
'D'	D	68	44
'E'	E	69	45

char	key	dec	hex
'F'	F	70	46
'G'	G	71	47
'H'	H	72	48
'I'	I	73	49
'J'	J	74	4A
'K'	K	75	4B
'L'	L	76	4C
'M'	M	77	4D
'N'	N	78	4E
'O'	O	79	4F
'P'	P	80	50
'Q'	Q	81	51
'R'	R	82	52
'S'	S	83	53
'T'	T	84	54
'U'	U	85	55
'V'	V	86	56
'W'	W	87	57
'X'	X	88	58
'Y'	Y	89	59
'Z'	Z	90	5A
'['	[	91	5B
'\'	\	92	5C
']'	]	93	5D
'^'	^	94	5E
'_'	_	95	5F
'`'	`	96	60
'a'	a	97	61
'b'	b	98	62
'c'	c	99	63
'd'	d	100	64
'e'	e	101	65
'f'	f	102	66
'g'	g	103	67
'h'	h	104	68
'i'	i	105	69
'j'	j	106	6A
'k'	k	107	6B
'l'	l	108	6C
'm'	m	109	6D

char	key	dec	hex
'n'	n	110	6E
'o'	o	111	6F
'p'	p	112	70
'q'	q	113	71
'r'	r	114	72
's'	s	115	73
't'	t	116	74
'u'	u	117	75
'v'	v	118	76
'w'	w	119	77
'x'	x	120	78
'y'	y	121	79
'z'	z	122	7A
'{'	{	123	7B
'!'	!	124	7C
'}'	}	125	7D
'~'	~	126	7E
DEL	del	127	7F

Appendix 2

asserta(clause)	/* Add clause to the top of the current database. */
assertz(clause)	/* Add clause to the bottom of the current database. */
attribute(A)	/* Assign or retrieve the default video attribute for all screen positions. */
back(X)	/* Move the graphics turtle in the opposite direction X steps. */
beep	/* Ring the console bell. */
bios(I,In,Out)	/* Invoke BIOS interrupt I at input register In, with output register Out. */
bound(X)	/* Check to see if X is bound. */
char_int(C,I)	/* Bind character C to integer I.*/
clearwindow	/* Clear interior of active window to spaces. */
closefile(synonym)	/* Close the disk file accessed as "synonym." */
comline(X)	/* Retrieves execution string X from the command line. */
config("dosfile.ext")	/* Loads disk file dosfile.ext as a program configuration file. */
consult("dosfile.ext")	/* Read the contents of the disk file dosfile.ext into the current program. */
cursor(R,C)	/* Position the cursor at row R, column C. */
cursorform(B,T)	/* Form cursor from bottom scanline B to top scanline T. */
date(YY,MM,DD)	/* Set or return system clock date to year YY, month MM, date DD. */
deletefile("dosfile.ext")	/* Erase disk file dosfile.ext from currently logged storage area. */
dir("\path","*.spc",Name")	/* Display the directory for path \path, filespec *.spc, and returns filename Name. */

(continued)

disk("d:\path")   /* Set default drive and directory
                                   path to d:\path. */

display(Text)   /* Display string Text in the
                                   active window. */

dot(R,C,Color)   /* Paint a dot at row R, column C
                                   in color Color. */

edit(Str1,Str2)   /* Invoke the built-in editor and
                                   edits string Str1 for output as
                                   string Str2. */

editmsg(I,O,L,R,M,H,P,C)   /* Invoke the built-in editor and
                                   edits string I for output as string
                                   O, with left header L, right header
                                   R, message M, help facility H,
                                   cursor position P, and termination
                                   code C). */

eof(synonym)   /* Monitor the end-of-file marker
                                   in file synonym. */

existfile("dosfile.ext")   /* Check to see if the disk file
                                   dosfile.ext resides in the
                                   currently logged storage area. */

exit   /* Exit from the current program
                                   to the Turbo Prolog menu. */

fail   /* Enforce backtracking at this
                                   point. */

field_attr(R,C,L,A)   /* Assign or retrieve values for
                                   a field at row R, column C in the
                                   current window, with length L and
                                   video attribute A. */

field_str(R,C,L,Str)   /* Write or retrieve string Str of
                                   length L at row R, column C. */

filemode(synonym,M)   /* Access file synonym
                                   in mode M
                                   (0 = text mode,
                                    1 = binary mode). */

filepos(synonym,P,M)   /* Monitor current position P in file
                                   synonym, with relation to mode M
                                   (0 = start of file,
                                    1 = current position,
                                    2 = end of file). */

file_str("dosfile.ext",X)   /* Read file string from
                                   dosfile.ext and bind to variable
                                   X; or write string X to file. */

findall(X,Pred,L)   /* Compile list L of values for X
                                   for the argument of predicate
                                   Pred. */

flush(synonym)   /* Flush file synonym to the
                                   current output destination. */

forward(X)   /* Move the graphics turtle in its
                                current direction X steps. */

free(X)   /* Check to see if X is unbound. */

frontchar(Str,C,T)   /* Segregate string Str into front
                                character C and tail T. */

frontstr(N,Str1,Str2,Str3)   /* Segregate string Str1 into two
                                strings, with Str2 containing the
                                first N characters of Str1, and
                                Str3 containing the remainder. */

fronttoken(Str,T,Trail)   /* Segregate string Str into token
                                T and trail Trail. */

gotowindow(W)   /* Transfer control rapidly to
                                window W, without screen
                                buffering. */

graphics(M,P,B)   /* Initialize the screen in
                                graphics mode M, with palette P
                                and background color B. */

isname(Str)   /* Check to see if the contents
                                of string Str is a reserved or
                                restricted Turbo Prolog name. */

keypressed   /* Check to see if a key has been
                                pressed. */

left(D)   /* Rotate the current direction of
                                the graphcis turtle D degrees to
                                the left.

line(R1,C1,R2,C2,P)   /* Draw a line from the point at
                                row R1, column C1 to the point at
                                row R2, column C2, in color P. */

makewindow(N,S,F,T,R,C,H,W)   /* Construct a window with window
                                number N, screen video attribute
                                S, frame video attribute F, header
                                text T, at row R, column C, with
                                a height of H rows and a width of
                                W columns. */

membyte(S,O,B)   /* Store or get byte B at segment
                                S with offset value O. */

memword(S,O,W)   /* Store or get word W at segment
                                S with offset value O. */

nl   /* Output a carriage return (new
                                line character). */

not(clause)   /* Negates success or failure of
                                a clause. */

(continued)

```
openappend(synonym,"dosfile.ext")    /* Open disk file dosfile.ext
                                         for appending, as synonym. */

openmodify(synonym,"dosfile.ext")    /* Open disk file dosfile.ext,
                                         for modifying, as synonym. */

openread(synonym,"dosfile.ext")      /* Open disk file dosfile.ext,
                                         for reading, as synonym. */

openwrite(synonym,"dosfile.ext")     /* Open disk file dosfile.ext,
                                         for writing, as synonym. */

pencolor(C)                          /* Use color C for drawing with the
                                         graphics turtle. */

pendown                              /* Start the graphics turtle's
                                         drawing action. */

penpos(R,C,D)                        /* Assign or retrieve the current
                                         row R, column C, and direction D
                                         of the graphics turtle. */

penup                                /* Terminate the graphics turtle's
                                         drawing action. */

portbyte(P,V)                        /* Send or get value V at port
                                         P. */

ptr_dword(Str,S,O)                   /* Get segment S and offset value
                                         O for string Str. */

readchar(C)                          /* Read character C from the
                                         current input stream. */

readdevice(synonym)                  /* Assign file synonym as the
                                         current input source. */

readint(I)                           /* Read integer I from the current
                                         input stream. */

readln(L)                            /* Read string line L from the
                                         current input stream. */

readreal(R)                          /* Read real number R from the
                                         current input stream. */

readterm(D,T)                        /* Read term T belonging to
                                         domain D from current input
                                         stream. */

removewindow                         /* Remove the active window. */

renamefile("name.1","name.2")        /* Rename DOS file name.1 to
                                         name.2. */

retract(clause)                      /* Retract a clause previously
                                         added to the database with asserta
                                         or assertz. */

right(D)                             /* Rotate the current direction of
                                         the graphics turtle D degrees. */
```

save("dosfile.ext")   /* Save the current database in the disk file <u>dosfile.ext</u>. */

scr_attr(R,C,A)   /* Assign video attribute A to the character at row R, column C. */

scr_char(R,C.Char)   /* Write or read character Char at row R, column C. */

shiftwindow(W)   /* Transfer screen operations to window number W. */

sound(L,F)   /* Produce an audio tone of F frequency for L hundredths of a second. */

storage(S,H,T)   /* Retrieve the available stack S, heap H, and trail T. */

str_char(Str,Char)   /* Bind single-character string Str to character Char. */

str_int(Str,Int)   /* Bind string Str to decimal equivalent Int. */

str_len(Str,L)   /* Determine length L of string Str. */

str_real(Str,R)   /* Bind string Str to real number R. */

system("command")   /* Access DOS and execute the command string command. */

text   /* Set all screen positions to text mode. */

time(HH,MM,SS,00)   /* Set system clock to hour HH, minute MM, second SS, hundredths 00. */

trace(T)   /* Toggle compiler trace function to status T (on or off). */

upper_lower(Str1,Str2)   /* Bind upper case string Str1 to lower case string Str2. */

window_attr(A)   /* Assign attribute A to the the active window. */

window_str(Str)   /* Displays or reads string Str in the active window. */

write(S)   /* Write the string, value, or series of strings and values assigned to S to the current output stream. */

(continued)

Appendix 2

```
writedevice(synonym)            /* Assign synonym as the current
                                output destination. */

writef(Str,Obj,Obj...Obj)       /* Write formatted string Str, using
                                objects Obj, Obj..Obj.
                                (-% = justify left
                                 %  = justify right
                                 .D = decimals points D
                                 e  = exponential notation
                                 f  = fixed decimal
                                 g  = shortest format) */
```

total No. of built-in predicates = 90

Prolog-to-Turbo Prolog Conversion Chart

Prolog	Turbo Prolog
arg(N,T,A)	—
asserta(clause)	asserta(clause)
assertz(clause)	assertz(clause)
atom(A)	isname(A)
atomic(A)	str_int(A,I), isname(A)
clause(X,Y)	—
consult(file)	consult(file)
!	!
display(X)	display(X)
fail	fail
functor(T,F,N)	—
integer(I)	str_int(Str,I)
nl	findall(X,Pred,List)
nonvar(X)	nl
put(X)	free(X)
read(X)	write(X)
	readln(X)
	readchar(X)
	readint(X)
	readreal(X)
reconsult(file)	readterm(X)
repeat	(user-defined)
retract(clause)	—
see(file)	retract(clause)
	openread(file,"dosfile.ext"),
seeing(F)	readdevice(file)
seen(file)	readdevice(F)
set_of(X,atom,List)	closefile(file)
tab(X)	—

(continued)

Prolog	Turbo Prolog
tell(file)	openwrite(file,"dosfile.ext"), writedevice(file)
telling(F)	writedevice(F)
told(file)	closefile(file)
trace	trace(T)
var(X)	bound(X)
write(X)	write(X)

Turbo Prolog Predicate Flow Patterns

The left column lists the built-in Turbo Prolog predicates with the legal number of parameters which may appear in each respective argument.

The right column shows the valid flow patterns in which the parameters may be used.

Turbo Prolog Predicate	Permissible Argument Flow Patterns
asserta(X)	(in)
assertz(X)	(in)
	(out)
attribute(X)	(in)
	(out)
back(X)	(in)
bios(X,Y,Z)	(in,in,out)
bound(X)	(out)
char_int(X,Y)	(in,out)
	(out,in)
	(in,in)
closefile(X)	(in)
consult(X)	(in)
cursor(X,Y)	(in,in)
cursorform(X,Y)	(in,in)
date(X,Y,Z)	(in,in,in)
	(out,out,out)
deletefile(X)	(in)
dir(X,Y,Z)	(in,in,out)
disk(X)	(in)
	(out)
display(X)	(in)
dot(X,Y,Z)	(in,in,in)
	(in,in,out)
edit(X,Y)	(in,out)
editmsg(A,B,C,D,E,F,G)	(in,out,in,in,in,in,out)

Turbo Prolog Predicate	Permissible Argument Flow Patterns
eof(X)	(in)
existfile(X)	(in)
field_attr(A,B,C,D)	(in,in,in,in)
	(in,in,in,out)
field_str	(in,in,in,in)
	(in,in,in,out)
filepos(X,Y,Z)	(in,in,in)
	(in,out,in)
file_str(X,Y)	(in,out)
flush(X)	(in)
forward(X)	(in)
free(X)	(out)
frontchar(X,Y,Z)	(in,out,out)
	(in,in,out)
	(in,out,in)
	(in,in,in)
	(out,in,in)
frontstr(A,B,C,D)	(in,in,out,out)
fronttoken(X,Y,Z)	(in,out,out)
	(in,in,out)
	(in,out,in)
	(in,in,in)
	(out,in,in)
graphics(X,Y,Z)	(in,in,in)
isname(X)	(in)
left(X)	(in)
	(out)
line(A,B,C,D)	(in,in,in,in)
makewindow(A,B,C,D,E,F,G,H)	(in,in,in,in,in,in,in,in)

Turbo Prolog Predicate	Permissible Argument Flow Patterns
membyte(X,Y,Z)	(in,in,in)
	(in,in,out)
memword(X,Y,Z)	(in,in,in)
	(in,in,out)
openappend(X,Y)	(in,in)
openmodify(X,Y)	(in,in)
openread(X,Y)	(in,in)
openwrite(X,Y)	(in,in)
pencolor(X)	(in)
portbyte(X,Y)	(in,in)
	(in,out)
ptr_dword(X,Y,Z)	(in,out,out)
	(out,in,in)
readchar(X)	(out)
readdevice(X)	(in)
	(out)
readint(X)	(out)
readln(X)	(out)
readreal(X)	(out)
readterm(X,Y)	(out,in)
renamefile(X,Y)	(in,in)
retract(X)	(in)
right(X)	(in)
	(out)
save(X)	(in)
scr_attr(X,Y,Z)	(in,in,in)
	(in,in,out)

Turbo Prolog Predicate	Permissible Argument Flow Patterns
scr_char(X,Y,Z)	(in,in,in)
	(in,in,out)
shiftwindow(X)	(in)
	(out)
sound(X,Y)	(in,in)
storage(X,Y,Z)	(out,out,out)
str_char(X,Y)	(in,out)
	(out,in)
	(in,in)
str_int(X,Y,Z)	(in,out)
	(out,in)
	(in,in)
str_len(X,Y)	(in,in)
	(in,out)
str_real(X,Y)	(in,out)
	(out,in)
	(in,in)
system(X)	(in)
time(A,B,C,D)	(in,in,in,in)
	(out,out,out,out)
trace(X)	(in)
	(out)
upper_lower(X,Y)	(in,in)
	(in,out)
	(out,in)
window_attr(X)	(in)
window_str(X)	(in)
	(out)
write(X)	(in)
writedevice(X)	(in)
	(out)
writef(X,Y)	(in,in)

APPENDIX 5

Turbo Prolog Graphics/Sound Values

Monochrome Video Attributes

Display	Effect	Value
Normal	Normal	7
Normal	Underlined characters	8
Normal	High intensity characters	15
Normal	Blinking characters	135
Inverse	Normal	112
Inverse	Underlined characters	113
Inverse	High intensity characters	120
Inverse	Blinking characters	240

Color Video Attributes

Background							
	Black	0	Gray	8	Blue	16
	Lt. blue	24	Green	32	Lt. green	40
	Cyan	48	Red	64	Lt. red	72
	Magenta	80	Lt. mg.	88	Brown	96
	Yellow	104	White	112	Int. wht.	120

Foreground							
	Black	0	Blue	1	Green	2
	Cyan	3	Red	4	Magenta	5
	Brown	6	White	7		

Optional Turbo Prolog Graphics Modes

Adaptor	Screen	Colors	Resolution	Mode
Color/Graphics	Medium resolution	4	200 × 320	1
Color/Graphics	High resolution	Mono	200 × 640	2
Enhanced	Medium resolution	16	200 × 320	3
Enhanced	High resolution	16	200 × 640	4
Enhanced	Enhanced resolution	13	350 × 640	5

Background Color Values

Black	0	Blue	1	Green	2	Cyan	3
Red	4	Magenta	5	Brown	6	White	7
Gray	8	Lt. blue	9	Lt. green	10	Lt. cyan	11
Lt. red	12	Lt. magenta	13	Yellow	14	Intense white	15

Optional Pen Colors for the Graphics Turtle

Black	0	Blue	1
Green	2	Cyan	3
Red	4	Magenta	5
Brown	6	White	7

Frequencies of Common Notes

C	131	C	262	C	523	C	1047
D	147	D	294	D	587	D	1175
E	165	E	230	E	659	E	1319
F	175	F	349	F	698	F	1397
G	196	G	392	G	784	G	1568
A	220	A	440	A	880	A	1760
B	247	B	494	B	988	B	1976

Sample Tone Lengths for Various Tempos

Tempo	Tone Length
Larghissimo	150
Largo	100
Adagio	79
Andante	56
Moderato	50
Allegro	36
Presto	29

Appendix 5

Turbo Prolog Language Summary

Fact   relation(object,object...object)

$$\text{where predicate} = \text{relation}$$
$$\text{argument} = \text{(object,object...object)}$$

Examples:
```
patient(male,57)
wine(zinfandel,red)
moves(blk,pawn,k4)
book(author,title,pdate)
```

Object   object

Examples:
```
budget
    5000
    fixed_price
    "medical history"
    144
    3122.2
```

Compound
object

object(sub-object,sub-object...sub-object)

Examples:
```
suspected(Organism)
symptoms(inverted_st,chest_pain,elevated_sgot)
```

Functor

predicate(functor(subobject,subobject))

Symbol   symbol

Examples:
```
item
5012
account_number
"O-ring seal"
```

(continued)

String   "string"

Examples:

         "EKG tracing"
         "ischemia"
         "62 years old"

Char   'char'

Examples:

         'a'
         '/'
         '\ 13'

Integer $-32769 >$ integer < 32768

Examples:

         10
         512
         144

Real   real number

Examples:

         52580
         -94181
         67.05
         $-720e318$

File   synonym

Examples:

         datafile
         input
         screen
         keyboard

Relation   relation(object,object...object)

Examples:

         part(number,brand,descr,price)
         symptom(chest_pain,ischemia,elevated_sgot)
         stipulates(contract,fixed_price)

Variable   X

Known

Examples:

```
get(X)
find(Part)
compute(Price)
write(Action)
```

Anonymous
Example:

```
retract(get(_) )
```

Domain
declaration

object = domain

Example:
```
domains
      name = string
       sex = symbol
       age = integer
    weight = real
    record = file
```

Predicate
declaration

predicate(object,object...object)

Example:

```
predicates
     suspected(symbol)
     prediction
     record(name,sex,age,weight)
```

Global
predicate
declaration

predicate(object...object) — (f...f)(f...f)

Example:

```
global predicates
     patient(age,weight,blood_pressure)(i,i,i)(o,o,o)
```

(continued)

Appendix 6

Operators

Arithmetic

+	Add
−	Subtract
*	Multiply
/	Divide
mod	Remainder
div	Quotient
abs	Absolute value
arctan	Arctangent
cos	Cosine
exp	Exponent
ln	Natural logarithm
log	Logarithm
sin	Sin
sqrt	Square root
tan	Tangent

Relational

=	Equals
>	Is greater than
> =	Is greater than or equal to
<	Is less than
< =	Is less than or equal to
< >	Is not equal to

List

[member1,member2...memberN]

Examples:

[495,512,424,570]
["Kendhal","Smith","Larsen"]
[income,expenses,net,cash_flow]

Clause

(See fact and rule)

predicate(object,object...object).
conclusion(argument):-
            premise(argument).

Examples:

suspected(Organism).

symptoms(Symptom1,Symptom2,Symptom3).

recommendation(sell):-
            price(commodity,declined).

Rule

```
conclusion(argument):-
    premise1(argument),
    premise2(argument),
    .
    .
    .
    premiseN(argument).
```

Examples:

```
price(lumber,"will rise"):-
    supply(lumber,shortage).

display_text:-
    not(eof(document)),
    readln(Text),
    write(Text),nl,
    display_text.
```

Appendix 6

Turbo Prolog Compiler Directives

check_cmpio   /* Check for the existence of compound
                        input/out flow patterns. */

check_determ   /* Check determinism, and issue a
                        warning if any nondeterministic
                        clauses are found. */

code=nnnnn   /* Specify the code array size in paragraphs
                        of 16 bytes per paragraph. */

diagnostics   /* List summary of compiler diagnostics. */

include"filename"   /* Include the file filename on
                        compilation. */

nobreak   /* Ignore a Ctrl-Break or F6 key press
                        during execution. */

nowarnings   /* Omit all warning messages. */

shorttrace   /* Trace all predicates, without aborting
                        system optimizations. */

shorttrace p1,p2   /* Trace predicates p1 and p1 only,
                        without aborting system optimizations. */

trace   /* Trace all predicates, removing any
                        system optimizations. */

trace p1,p2   /* Trace predicates p1 and p2 only,
                        removing any system optimizations. */

trail=nnn   /* Specify the trail size in bytes. */

Index

NOTES

NOTES

NOTES

1-800 492 - 4531 Phila

237 - 2747 — Toll free

Rajesh   21 - 0   026   9.00

484

9.45 - 6.35 pm,

23rd 7.30 grade.